M000279405

gestalten

The MONOCLE
Travel Guide Series

Stockholm

For more information, please visit *gestalten.com*

Bibliographic information published by the Deutsche Nationalbibliothek: The Deutsche Nationalbibliothek lists this publication in the Deutsche Nationalbibliografie; detailed bibliographic data are available online at *dnb.d-nb.de*

This book was printed on paper certified by the FSC®

Monocle editor in chief and chairman: *Tyler Brûlé*
Monocle editor: *Andrew Tuck*
Books editor: *Joe Pickard*
Guide editor: *Josh Fehnert*

Designed by *Monocle*
Proofreading by *Monocle*
Typeset in *Plantin & Helvetica*

Printed by *Offsetdruckerei Grammlich, Pliezhausen*

Made in Germany

Published by *Gestalten*, Berlin 2017
ISBN 978-3-89955-904-0

Welcome
Seductive Stockholm

In recent years the global gaze has settled on *Stockholm*, drawn by its techy start-ups and world-beating fashion brands. But the city of 1.5 million souls has always been a quiet poster child for all that Nordic cities do best: accepting people, a *liberal lean* and a *beautiful backdrop*.

Despite its recent digital dalliance, the city itself remains an analogue delight. The Swedish capital occupies *14 pretty islands* straddled by 57 bridges that crisscross the Stockholm Archipelago and Lake Mälaren, which leads out to the Baltic Sea. The winters are admittedly long and chilly, which creates a few curious year-round conditions. For one, the interiors of restaurants and people's homes are just plain nicer than elsewhere (creating *a comfy nook* is a worthy investment if you spend half the year indoors).

The latitude also breeds a *lively appreciation for the sun* – when it rolls around – and there are few delights that compare to diving into the crystalline waters of the archipelago or sipping a sundowner aboard a gently bobbing boat. You can also add to the mix a glut of *world-class galleries*, one-off restaurants (that serve decent portions and leave out the fuss – New Nordic movement take note) and retail to rival any city on Earth.

Visually Stockholm is a hodgepodge of chocolate-box buildings and *cobbled lanes*, plus tasteful townhouses, contemporary infrastructure and a smattering of *church spires*. Join us on a tour – by foot, boat and taxi (or the efficient underground T-bana) – of this *most charming* of northern European beauties. — (M)

Contents
—— Navigating the city

Use the key below to help navigate the guide section by section.

Hotels

Food and drink

Retail

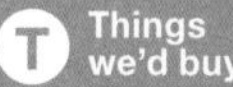
Things we'd buy

Essays

C Culture

D Design and architecture

S Sport and fitness

W Walks

Map
Waterway wandering

Stockholm was first settled on the central island of Gamla Stan (Old Town) but the need for space soon saw the city spread north to eclectic Norrmalm, south to now-hip Södermalm, east to leafy Djurgården and chic Östermalm, and west to residential Kungsholmen. These neighbourhoods remain the essential co-ordinates for understanding the capital today – although Vasastan (north of Norrmalm) is also well worth adding to the address book.

Despite the fact that the many attractions here are scattered across pretty waterways, Stockholm's small scale makes it surprisingly simple to conquer on foot. The city is teeming with taxis but the three-line metro (called the T-bana) is fast, efficient and has excellent platform-side art at which to gawp (*see page 120*).

Lastly, don't leave town without hopping on a ferry. Head to Nybroviken or Slussen for services to the Djurgården (east) or Hammarby Sjöstad (south). All aboard.

Stockholm Arlanda Airport
Vanadislunden
VASASTAN
Public Library
Bromma Stockholm Airport
Vasaparken
Sven-Harrys Konstmuseum
KUNGSHOLMEN
Concert H
Kronobergsparken
Waterfront Conference Centre
Cen Stat
Stockholm Court House
Rålambshovsparken
City Hall
Mälaren
Riddarholmen C
Drottningholm Palace
Mariat
Färgfabriken
SÖDERMALM
Stockholm International Fairs

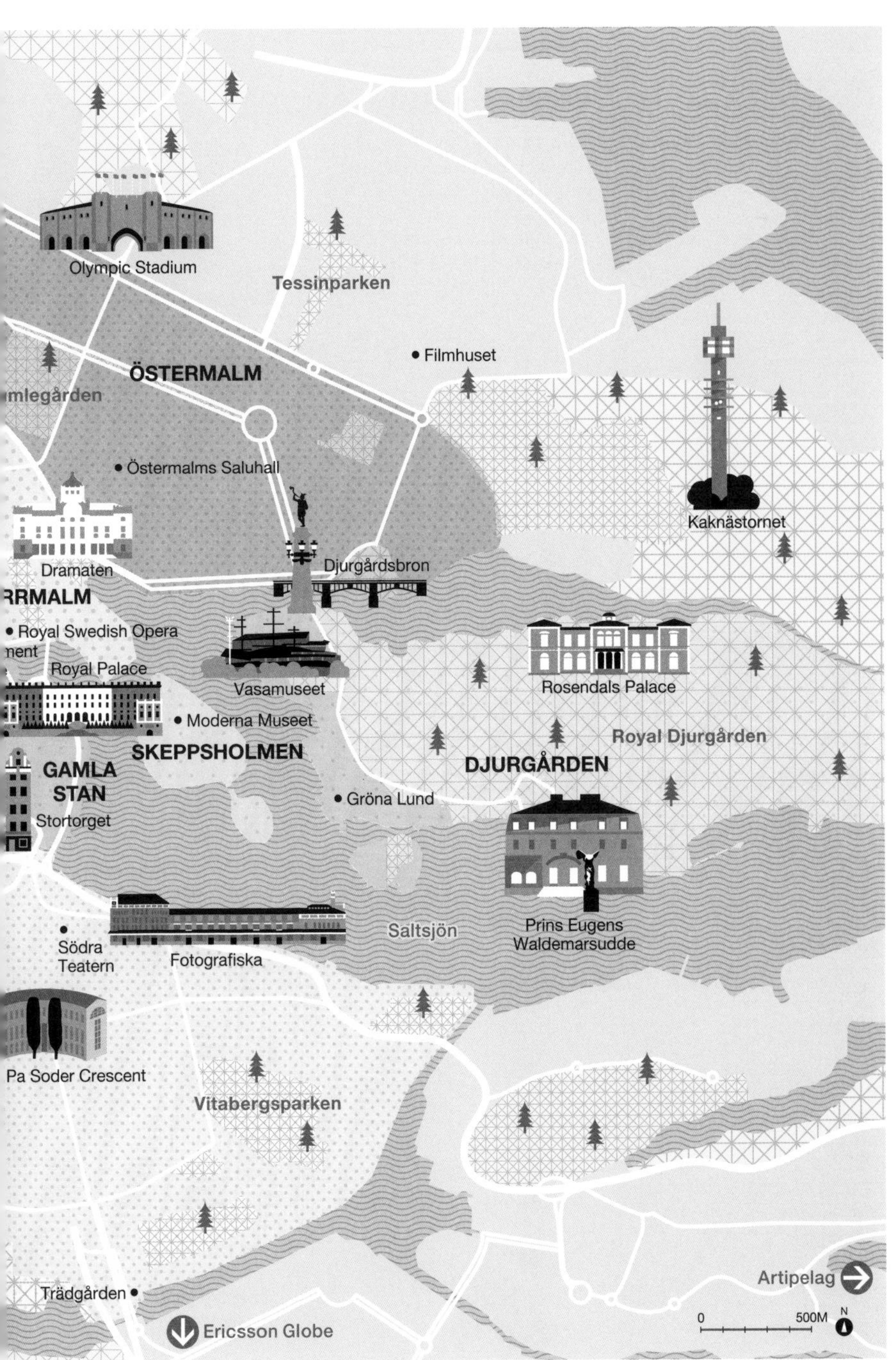
Olympic Stadium
Tessinparken
Filmhuset
ÖSTERMALM
mlegården
Östermalms Saluhall
Kaknästornet
Dramaten
Djurgårdsbron
RRMALM
Royal Swedish Opera
nent
Royal Palace
Vasamuseet
Rosendals Palace
Moderna Museet
Royal Djurgården
SKEPPSHOLMEN
GAMLA
STAN
DJURGÅRDEN
Gröna Lund
Stortorget
Saltsjön
Prins Eugens
Waldemarsudde
Södra
Teatern
Fotografiska
Pa Soder Crescent
Vitabergsparken
Artipelag
Trädgården
0
500M
N
Ericsson Globe

Need to know
— Stockholm staples

Stockholmers are an accepting bunch but it's always best to be informed when visiting somewhere new. From transport to tipping, etiquette to opening hours, these quick facts will help you navigate the city.

Conversation
Talking points

Swedes are for the most part flawless (yet occasionally shy) English speakers; be patient and polite and you will be understood. One quirk among residents, however, is a proclivity to inhale in a short burst when you're talking (the sound is akin to a sharp gasp). Don't worry, you haven't inadvertently shocked your interlocutor: this is a custom, particularly among those who hail from the north, that simply means "Yes" or "I'm listening". Keep going.

Seasons
Hot and cold

Stockholm's northern latitude has done much to shape the city's culture. The winters are long and cold so shop and restaurant owners naturally spend more – and more judiciously – on appealing interiors. Summers, by contrast, are effervescent, short and celebrated (droves of workers will congregate in sunny corners on their lunch breaks). A word to the wise: pack for the season. Many first-timers arrive with clothing that is ill suited for the throes of extreme weather.

Transport
Cab concerns

Amazingly, considering the nation's highly developed legal system and tight regulations in other affairs, taxis are unregulated in Sweden, so a company can choose to charge you whatever it likes per kilometre. Visitors should either look up and call a specific company or hail an app-powered alternative (you know the ones). Do also make use of the art-studded and efficient metro, T-bana, or walk if you can spare the time. Stockholm is a simple city to navigate by foot despite its numerous islands, bridges and waterways.

Money matters
To their credit

The city may be too technology savvy for its own good on this front; whipping out cash is often treated as an anachronism, as if you've tried to pay for your morning paper with livestock or a piece of Viking hack-silver. Tap-and-go card payment is therefore ubiquitous. Most taxis allow you to pay with plastic, as do a surprising proportion of shops and restaurants (even the older-looking ones).

Cityscape
Style council

Stockholm's good looks are assured by its natural beauty (granite islands awash in a preternaturally calm archipelago see to that) but the built side of things is firmly monitored by city hall. The so-called Beauty Council – officially Rådet till Skydd för Stockholms Skönhet (Council for the Protection of the Beauty of Stockholm) – ensures that new-builds don't overshadow or clash with existing treasures. Although the body has copped criticism for its conservatism and the lengthy deliberations that it undertakes, it's heartening to know that someone's safeguarding the city's handsome appearance.

Tip-top restaurants
Change of scene

When it comes to tipping, it's standard to leave up to 10 per cent. For the rundown of the city's best restaurants, cafés and bars see our recommendations (*page 26*), which range from homely establishments offering *husmanskost* (comfort food) to fresh openings. If you're keen to try the handiwork of the city's finest chefs without the hefty pricetag there are two alternatives. Bakfickan (literally "back pocket") is the smaller, cheaper sibling of the grand Operakällaren restaurant, one of the city's most celebrated spots. Likewise Teatern at Ringen Centrum in Södermalm is a food court in which some of the city's best chefs riff on the popularity of street food with affordable but nonetheless delicious fare.

Parental leave
Kiddy care

Sweden offers new parents (male as well as female) generous and equitable maternity leave to a degree that's hard to fathom in other countries. Parents get 480 days of leave in total, up to half of which can be claimed by dad. As such Stockholm's cafés host as many dishy daddies as they do yummy mummies with their tots.

Home comforts
Sweet talk

The Danes have *hygge*, an untranslatable sensation akin to comfiness that has taken Sunday supplements and bestseller lists by storm. The Swedes, however, have *fika*. The practice (which you can read more about on page 79) is that of holing up with an acquaintance, sipping coffee and nibbling on something sweet. The merits of both are many but the chance of a Swede admitting that the Danes have a cultural monopoly on cosiness? Zilch.

Timings
Call it a day

Most cultural attractions, shops and some restaurants close on Mondays, so do check in advance. On Fridays (as on most days compared with western European countries) the Swedes finish work early and many dine at about 17.00 or 18.00, so you should also factor this into your plans. One alternative is a Wednesday meet-up. Colloquially known as Lillördag or "Little Saturday", the midweek mark is fair game for a swift dinner and drink and many bars and restaurants are pleasingly full as a result.

Etiquette
Bare truths

Stockholmers are liberal and laidback. A hug is preferred to a kiss on first meeting (though of course a shake is sometimes required in more formal circles) and straight talking preferred to the more dramatic greetings common in southern Europe. What may on first impressions appear to be standoffishness usually evaporates quickly to give way to friendliness. One situation in which the Swedes are said to break their cover is when it comes to nudity (though this has become a little overstated as it's been repeated). Whether it's a summer dip in the lake or sweating it out in a sauna, the Swedes are usually unabashed when it comes to letting it all hang out.

Hotels
Swedish stop-ins

A recent land-grab has reignited competition in Stockholm's once-stuffy hotel scene. Two 2017 openings in the same once-unloved square set a high benchmark but add an island escape, an adorable converted residence plus a few rebooted city-centre options and you'll find stays to suit the most discerning of visitors.

For years Stockholm's stopovers lagged listlessly behind its shops, restaurants and museums in terms of charm: passé, never classy and with a few too many threadbare throwbacks. However, we're pleased to report that this is no longer the case. Speaking of which, may we give you a hand with yours?

①
Ett Hem, Lärkstaden
Home Swede Home

Ett Hem (A Home) is Stockholm's finest hotel. The Ilse Crawford-designed space mingles modern swish, antiques, books, tasteful furniture and tactile finishes, with the most pleasing results. Sit down in the restaurant and breakfast appears, or wander into the kitchen and pop your head in the fridge before chatting with the chef about what you're after.

Owner Jeanette Mix (*pictured*) opened the hotel in 2012; today she and her staff hold themselves to the highest standards of thoughtfulness and charm. Each of the 12 rooms (yes, just 12 – book ahead) is decorated uniquely: Swedish oak and sheepskin throws; a parquet floor here, a colourful rug there. They combine with planters, Scandinavian chairs and sink-in sofas to create the most superb of stays. The rub? Well, Lärkstaden is a 10 or 15-minute amble from the city proper, a huge distance by the standards of this small city.
2 Sköldungagatan, 114 27
+46 (0)8 200 590
etthem.se

MONOCLE COMMENT: Swedish landscape gardener Ulf Nordfjell's outdoor terrace is a lovely, leafy place in which to unwind.

2

Hobo, Norrmalm
Wanderer's rest

Hobo riffs on being a home for itinerants but with none of the implied scruffiness. One in a brace of new openings from Norwegian developer Petter Stordalen, this spot on Brunkebergstorg Square was built as a bank in the 1970s and Berlin-based designer Werner Aisslinger took on the task of giving the place its clean look. The 201 rooms (one a suite) feature wooden pegboard walls – holding Swedish-made goodies for sale – plus comfy Malmö-made beds from Hilding Anders.

Roof-restaurant Tak is great for sunnier days but the ground and first-floor bar and bistro is best during a cold snap. The touch is light here, compared with the ritzier atmosphere of next door's At Six (*see page 18*), which is under the same ownership. But don't let the playful jungle-inspired wallpaper and frivolity fool you: service is solicitous and the rooms superb (if bijou on occasion).
4 Brunkebergstorg, 111 51
+46 (0)8 5788 2700
hobo.se

MONOCLE COMMENT: Stockholm is easily traversed on two wheels; just borrow a Swedish-made Vélosophy bike from reception and see.

3

At Six, Norrmalm
Tasteful number

Named after its street number on Brunkebergstorg Square, At Six is sleeker than most hotels – all marble, tinted mirrors and a vast collection of contemporary art. It's kitted out by UK firm Universal Design Studio (of Edward Barber and Jay Osgerby's stable) and your first impressions will be dominated by the vast granite staircase with leather-clad handrails.

Upstairs are 343 rooms (43 of them suites) all in a sooty palette, with long emerald-coloured Carrara marble desks and Alcantara wardrobes that the designers were told to make capacious enough to hold a Nobel Gala gown (that's the intended audience questions answered then).

The first-floor restaurant ranges from bar seats to a 30-person dining table. There are also seven meeting rooms, a recording studio and a listening room for vinyl-lovers.
6 Brunkebergstorg, 111 51
+46 (0)8 5788 2800
hotelatsix.com

MONOCLE COMMENT: The so-called Listening Lounge comes complete with a Tokyo-built KRS speaker and a handmade Condesa mixer from Australia to complement the wheels of steel from Technics.

④

Hotel Skeppsholmen, Skeppsholmen
Never mind the barracks

Many of the pastel-hued buildings that make up this 78-room hotel are former military barracks that were built in 1699. Södermalm firm Claesson Koivisto Rune has preserved the finishes and dimensions (hence the modular bathrooms incorporated into the rooms without permanent walls).

Several rooms once housed bunks for multiple soldiers but today they afford space and calm: modern touches such as lamps by Achille Castiglioni and Pio Manzù for Flos sit tastefully in the age-old rooms. The tennis court outside dates from the days of Oscar II. As for food, chef Magnus Johansson's breakfast is the toast of the town.
1 Gröna gången, 111 86
+46 (0)8 407 2300
hotelskeppsholmen.se

MONOCLE COMMENT: One meeting room has a pawprint that was left in wet concrete in the 17th century.

5

Lydmar Hotel, Norrmalm
Varied spaces

Hop up the short flight of stairs to the book-peppered lobby of Pelle Lydmar's waterfront crowd-pleaser and you'll survey an artsy crowd enjoying chef Lelle Rössler's fine French and Swedish fare in the 50-cover dining room. Keep an eye out for the changing photography exhibitions in the lobby too.

The Lydmar Hotel was once the offices of a museum but now its five floors host rooms that range from the daringly designy to the classy and understated (there are 46 in total and one suite). A rooftop terrace, meanwhile, offers stunning views over the water towards the Old Town.
2 Södra Blasieholmshamnen, 103 24
+46 (0)8 223 160
lydmar.com

MONOCLE COMMENT: The Lydmar Hotel is operated by the nearby Grand Hôtel Stockholm so access to the Gotland-granite finery of the Grand's fitness centre is a bonus.

6

Winery Hotel, Solna
Rare vintage

Its far-flung location may be tough on guests who like to be in the thick of things (it's a 20-minute drive north of town) but the Winery Hotel is worth a stay for its service and curious conception.

Opened in 2016, it makes some 8,000 bottles of wine a year. Enjoy a glass in one of the hotel restaurants (Vinoteque, Winery Kitchen and a shop, Terreno Deli), overseen by Michel Jamais and chef Markus Gustafsson; then there's the rooftop bar with its own pool. The building itself is industrial with exposed brickwork but the rooms have dim lighting and soft accents by design agency Southeast.
20 Rosenborgsgatan, 169 74
+46 (0)8 146 000
thewineryhotel.se

MONOCLE COMMENT: The 184-room project is the shared dream of the Söder and Ruhne families, who between them also own a vineyard in Tuscany.

⑦

Haymarket by Scandic, Norrmalm

Art deco delight

Saved by the Scandic chain from the ignominy of being a second-rate department store, Haymarket opened in 2016. Inside, the 19th-century building is all art deco and chatter; the hum is from an excellent restaurant and bakery called Gretas (actress Greta Garbo worked here when it was a shop).

There are calmer berths on the mezzanine and another restaurant on the first floor called Paul's, after the owner of the erstwhile shop. A barstool at chef Gustav Onnermark's American brasserie is an excellent choice for lunch.

13-15 Hötorget, 111 57
+46 (0)8 5172 6700
scandichotels.com

MONOCLE COMMENT: Finding the 405 modern rooms can be complicated: the renovation spans five buildings. A short staircase or step informs you when you're crossing from one to another.

⑧
Nobis Hotel, Norrmalm
Top location

Nobis sits on the equivalent of London's Park Lane or Mayfair: Norrmalmstorg Square. Its 201 rooms are generous in size and festooned with dark-wood floors, comfy Duxiana beds and Carrara marble bathrooms.

Architecture firm Claesson Koivisto Rune converted the once-open courtyard into a vast six-storey central atrium and lounge area, presided over by two domed skylights and an Orrefors crystal chandelier the size of a small planet. Food comes courtesy of ground-floor restaurant Caina, a fresh-feeling Italian bistro overseen by chef Jacopo Braga.
2-4 Norrmalmstorg, 111 86
+46 (0)8 614 1000
nobishotel.se

MONOCLE COMMENT: Try the gin-based Basil Smash cocktail in the Guldbaren (Gold Bar). More than 85,000 have been made since the hotel's 2011 opening.

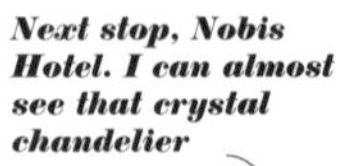

⑨
Hotel Diplomat, Östermalm
VIP treatment

The Hotel Diplomat is art nouveau in style (it was built in 1911) and overlooks the waters of Nybroviken Bay on well-to-do Strandvägen. Outside, the place is postcard-pretty, its red-tiled roof, claret awnings and hoisted flags all making for a magisterial sense of arrival. On the left as you enter (and after descending a short flight of steps; the building was converted from an embassy in 1962 and there are a few such sets to contend with) you'll arrive at the swish reception-cum-restaurant. The breakfast is excellent, particularly the omelette with gruyère.

Unusually the route up to the 130 rooms is almost as enjoyable as the chambers themselves, all elegant, airy and homely. Opt to take either the stunning marble staircase with carved wooden detailing and gold balustrades or an equally grandiose lift (a better choice if you're heading to the uppermost of the six floors).
7C Strandvägen, 114 56
+46 (0)8 459 6800
diplomathotel.com

MONOCLE COMMENT: The soft Portuguese cotton is exclusive to the Diplomat – you can buy it from reception.

⑩

Grand Hôtel, Norrmalm

Classic for a reason

This plush old hotel has hosted Nobel Laureates, notables and the ne'er-do-wells for 130 years or so – and the slightly dated grandeur aside, it's reassuringly friendly. All 280 rooms are well appointed but try to nab one renovated by Dap or Eye Studio in 2016 for something fresher and more design-minded. The pretty Cadier Bar downstairs is named after the building's architect and is great whether or not you're a guest; for something more substantial, chef Mathias Dahlgren is on hand to cater.

The Rutabaga restaurant is vegetarian and the colourfully tiled Matbaren an informal affair, while the ground-floor Grand Café and street-facing Veranda round out the excellent drinking and dining options. Plus, the subterranean Nordic Spa and Gym is a gem if you fancy a rubdown and a dip.

8 Södra Blasieholmshamnen, 103 27
+46 (0)8 679 3500
grandhotel.se

MONOCLE COMMENT: When the hotel opened in 1874 its architecture was a nod to the Royal Palace. To the king's embarrassment, however, the hotel had more flushing loos than his own abode (two to his one).

(11)

Hotel Kungsträdgården, Norrmalm
Old bank, new tricks

Located down a cobbled street that feels as if it's frozen in time, this 98-key independent has a quiet air considering its city-centre berth. The building, which was once a bank, is 250 years old but in 2015 the courtyard was clad in glass and transformed into the vast atrium that accommodates the lobby today.

The Swedish-French brasserie Makalös takes pride of place here, with 75 covers downstairs and another 100 on the mezzanine (there's also a plant-covered wall that snakes up four storeys to the skylights). Most of the floors and walls are original but Oslo-based Link Arkitektur has decked the place out in the Gustavian style (Swedish glam with Gallic gall, as King Gustav liked it) and added a few nice touches such as Jensen beds. Room 417 is the original prototype on which the others were modelled and remains our favourite.
11B Västra Trädgårdsgatan, 111 53
+46 (0)8 440 6650
hotelkungstradgarden.se

MONOCLE COMMENT: One remnant of the building's past use as a bank remains locked in the basement: a 1,500kg vault door that was too heavy to remove and still hosts the wine cellar.

12

Miss Clara Hotel, Normalm
Too cool for a school

The all-conquering Nobis group has five hotels in Stockholm, three featuring in our rundown; this one feels younger and hipper than the others. From the enthusiastic DJ-turned-MD Morsi Khaled to his smart staff who preside over the 80-cover downstairs restaurant (tastefully kitted out with Tärnsjö leather finishes and lamps made of decanters suspended from curtain rails), this feels like a spot designed for the local media set.

The interior has been given a makeover by Swedish architect Gert Wingårdh. Upstairs the rooms are tasteful, with dark parquet floors, woollen throws from Klippan and Byredo amenities. The ground-floor Giro pizzeria is a collaboration with the Da Michele pizzeria and serves Neapolitan-style delights to be enjoyed either at the bar, a stripped-back wooden table or an intimate banquette.
48 Sveavägen, 111 34
+46 (0)8 440 6700
missclarahotel.com

MONOCLE COMMENT: The 92-room hotel is named after Clara Strömberg, who presided over the place when it was a girl's school from 1910 until the 1930s.

Clean slate
The rooms are beautifully understated

Three more hotels

01 **Hotel Drottning Kristina, Östermalm:** A haven of 19th-century splendour at a reasonable price, this 101-key hotel mixes the Gustavian style with white walls, soft finishes and a few airy touches. Stureplan Square isn't far away; nor is leafy Humlegården Park.
hoteldrottningkristinastureplan.se

02 **Residence Perseus, Gamla Stan:** Hidden down an undulating street that's roughly the width of a hatchback, this pied-à-terre is equidistant from Stortorget Square, the Royal Palace and Nobel Museet – smack in the middle of the Old Town. The serviced apartments aren't catered and the building is a lesson in the topsy-turvy topography of the area: the entrance is on Baggensgatan but the back door is down two flights of stairs on cobbled Österlånggatan.
residenceperseus.com

03 **Berns Hotel, Norrmalm:** What started as the city's favourite music hall in the 1870s (and went on to host the likes of Diana Ross) welcomed a hotel a century later. While the turn-of-the-century style remains, the 80-plus rooms are invariably up to date with plush textiles, marble finishes and plenty of light. The music hall is still Stockholmers' go-to for a grand night out; the gilded and chandeliered dining room is one of the finest in Europe; and the terrace bar sees a flattering footfall almost year round.
berns.se

Food and drink
Step up to the plate

Clichés notwithstanding, Stockholm's culinary scene really does dish up a smörgåsbord of delights on the dining table. Contrary to the image painted by the worthy-at-times New Nordic movement (forage this, foam that) there's a likeable focus on hearty and informal meals that comes from a tradition of *husmanskost* (home food).

Alongside staples such as meatballs and *skagen* toast (brioche with mayo, egg and prawns) there is, of course, a batch of star chefs with smart new restaurants. There are also beautiful bakeries at which to *fika* – enjoy something sweet and baked with a coffee – and plenty of cafés in which to unwind. Join us for a taste of the best that Stockholm has to offer.

Restaurants
Eat up

1
PA&Co, Östermalm
Café culture

This pocket-sized bistro started more as a hangout when five pals bought the space in 1986 to host their friends and family. Though it quickly grew in popularity, the intimacy is undimmed and the food as delectable as ever (it even released a cookbook in 2016 to mark the 30-year milestone).

Dishes range from Swedish staples such as *råraka* (hash browns) and gravlax to simple continental plates, many inspired by Sweden's longstanding dalliance with French cuisine. The whole grilled sea bass is worth every krona.

8 Riddargatan, 114 35
+46 (0)8 611 0845
paco.se

Victory for veggies

Chef Mathias Dahlgren recently opened vegetarian restaurant Rutabaga in the Grand Hôtel on the Norrmalm waterfront. For a cheaper way to sample his fare try bakery Green Rabbit, which supplies his restaurant with baked goodies.
grandhotel.se; greenrabbit.se

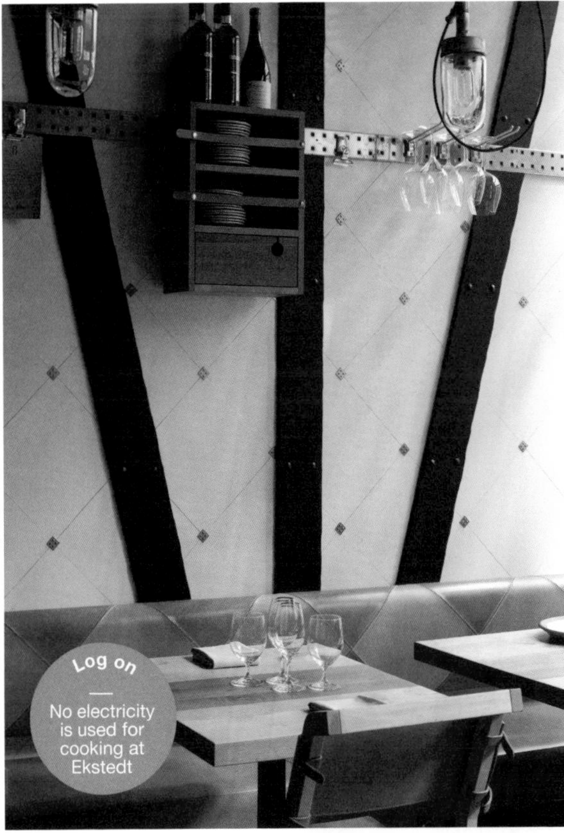

No electricity is used for cooking at Ekstedt

②
Ekstedt, Östermalm
All fired up

Your first clue that Ekstedt is unlike other restaurants comes as you notice wood smoke in the air. The kitchen only uses electricity for lighting and refrigeration, with birch logs providing all the heat for cooking. But this is no barbecue joint. Niklas Ekstedt takes inspiration from centuries-old Swedish techniques in a thoroughly modern way (expect reindeer with roe and charcoal cream or juniper-baked turbot). The room has lots of wood, leather and brass but don't be fooled: this is one of the most adventurous restaurants in town.
17 Humlegårdsgatan, 114 46
+46 (0)8 611 1210
ekstedt.nu

③
Sushi Sho, Vasastan
On a roll

The food at this lively sushi bar is as no-nonsense as the decor. "I wanted to create a place with Edomae-style, traditional Tokyo sushi; a few years ago all you could find here was fusion food," says founder and head chef Carl Ishizaki (*pictured*). He cooked for Japanese restaurants in Stockholm for more than 20 years before setting up shop.

Book in for one of three sittings (17.00, 19.00 or 21.00), where you'll be presented with a tasting menu of about 15 portions. They are served piece by piece at the wooden counter next to the chefs.
45 Upplandsgatan, 113 28
+46 (0)8 303 030
sushisho.se

4

Sturehof, Östermalm
Go fish

The waiters here may wear double-breasted jackets but the mood is more bustling brasserie than anything formal. Fresh seafood is the order of the day, although this city favourite started as a German beer hall back in 1897 before restaurateur PG Nilsson and the PA&Co gang (*see page 26*) acquired it.

Don't fear the extensive menu: perhaps start with some *knäckebröd*, then half a dozen oysters followed by deep-fried perch from the waters of Lake Mälaren. You can dawdle over that last glass of wine as the place is open till 02.00.
2 Stureplan, 114 35
+46 (0)8 440 5730
sturehof.com

Where to have 'husmanskost'

Husmanskost (home cooking) grew from working-class kitchens putting out filling plates to keep workers moving in winter. Such dishes became popular over the centuries and remain staples today. You'll often see a slim Swede put away a plate of meatballs that might trouble a larger person, such is the appetite for the classic fare.

01 **Lisa Elmqvist, Östermalm:** Brothers Ulf and Peter Elmqvist focus on seafood as their great-grandmother Lisa did in the 1920s. *Skagen* toast makes for a light-ish lunch and the hot dishes include whole lemon sole fried in garlic and parsley, served at tables draped in chequered tablecloths in a bustling atmosphere. *lisaelmqvist.se*

02 **Blå Dörren, Södermalm:** Behind the diminutive entrance (the name is literally "Blue Door") is a sizeable dining room and bar. Perched on dark wooden chairs and surrounded by copper pots, guests eagerly await a plate of smoked salmon with dill and potatoes or elk meatballs with a side of lingonberries. Wash it all down with a glass of the in-house Blå Dörren lager. *bla-dorren.se*

03 **Prinsen, Norrmalm:** *Husmanskost* can be served at a ferocious pace but Prinsen is a slower affair. While higher-end in execution, the atmosphere is never too formal. Call ahead to book a booth and opt for one of the house specials, such as the cod loin with baked egg yolk and cauliflower. *restaurangprinsen.eu*

5

AG, Kungsholmen

Meat your maker

Dining on a sleepy street in Kungsholmen may seem like the quiet option but this restaurant is always busy. The exterior isn't the most inviting but the Jonas Bohlin-designed interior (and legs of jamón) makes up for any wrongs.

Meat is the house speciality – the classic entrecôte and porterhouse, sourced from Swedish cattle, are supreme – but chef Håkan Matseus ensures there's plenty on the menu for all tastes, such as the cauliflower, Monte Enebro cheese and truffle gnocchi.

37 Kronobergsgatan, 112 33
+46 (0)8 4106 8100
restaurangag.se

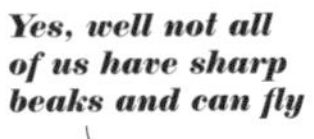

6

Oaxen Slip, Djurgården

Sail away

Agneta Green and Magnus Ek moved from Oaxen to set up shop in this former boatyard in 2013. The menu is a combination of Nordic recipes with a few ingredients from further afield: the lamb shoulder with yoghurt and turmeric sauce alone is worth the journey.

Chef Emil Grönlund is exacting when it comes to ingredients – he paces Oaxen's vegetable garden for broad beans, black radish and onions – and equally careful thought has gone into the decor. The adjoining Oaxen Krog serves a two-Michelin-starred tasting menu.

26 Beckholmsvägen, 115 21
+46 (0)8 5515 3105
oaxen.com

Babette, Vasastan

Pizza perfection

In Sweden, it's common to call a restaurant after an animal so owner Johan Agrell put a neon rooster in the window. However, he named the place after writer Karen Blixen's character Babette, who introduces French cuisine to Scandinavia.

The quirky signage is now iconic in Vasastan, whose residents flock here for a delectable marriage of Italian, French and Swedish food. The pizzas are as good as their Neapolitan rivals and best prefaced with lemoned-almonds and a glass of wine from Agrell's sizeable cellar.

6 Roslagsgatan, 113 55
+46 (0)8 5090 2224
babette.se

(8)
Gro, Vasastan
Green light

Behind a silver counter, young chef-owners Magnus Villnow and Henrik Norén (*both pictured, Villnow on left*) serve just eight dishes split into two four-course menus: Omnivor and Vegivor (the duo are renowned for their prowess with greens). Both finish with a delectable rhubarb, cream and cardamom combination.

Yes, the food is fancy but it's wholesome and the place itself is unfussy. *Gro* means "to sprout" but, while this haunt is growing on everyone, the small dining room isn't so book well in advance.
67 Sankt Eriksgatan, 113 32
+46 (0)8 643 4222
grorestaurang.se

Porky particulars

The Günters sausage stand, founded by Günter Schwarz, has been going strong since the 1980s; though he died in 2007, his name lives on. There are 20 varieties, including Tyrolean wurst, Spanish merquez and Polish bratwurst.
66 Karlbergsvägen, 113 35

Best for beer

01 **Omnipollos Hatt, Södermalm:** A simple affair with more small-batch beers than seats; the in-house Perikles pilsner is our draught of choice. It also serves sourdough pizza if you're peckish.
omnipolloshatt.com

02 **Akkurat, Södermalm:** As well known for its live music as its more than 200 beers (and 400 malt whiskies). The on-tap favourite is Södermalms Pilsner.
akkurat.se

03 **Tritonia, Gamla Stan:** This sophisticated space has a well-thought-through beer selection. Struggling to pick one? Tap Johan Thor for a tasting session.
tritonia.se

Operakällaren, Norrmalm
Sing for your supper

If Figaro's marriage isn't to your taste then forgo the opera itself for the dramatic restaurant downstairs. The art nouveau interior is decked out with gilded chandeliers and pastoral paintings in the main hall and a stained-glass vault in the bar, which was built in 1895 and became the go-to for turn-of-the-century intelligentsia.

In the 1960s the restaurant was refurbished by architect Peter Celsing and, in 1961, it began catering for royal banquets – an honour that chef Stefano Catenacci still holds today. He serves a European menu of both Swedish staples (try the reindeer fillet) and continental classics, paired with a superb wine list.

For a more casual experience, drop into Bakfickan ("Back Pocket"), a lower-key bistro attached to the main restaurant.
Operahuset, Karl XII:s Torg, 118 86
+46 (0)8 676 5800
operakallaren.se

⑩
Agrikultur, Vasastan
Field trip

Vasastan has recently emerged as a thrilling culinary quarter, with Agrikultur leading the pack. At first glance it's an unexpected success: small (just 24 seats), not much to look at from the outside and closed on weekends. But what sets it apart is the food.

Filip Fastén (former winner of Sweden's Cook of the Year contest) and Joel Åhlin change the set menu daily, depending on what's available from farmers in the vicinity. Together they create extraordinary dishes with roots in traditional Swedish cooking.

The vegetables are the stars; meat is relegated to a supporting role. Reservations can be hard to come by but the four best seats in the house, from which you can sit and watch the chefs at work, are kept for drop-ins.

43 Roslagsgatan, 113 54
+46 (0)8 150 202
agrikultur.se

Ilse, Vasastan
Swede dreams

Ilse may drape its tables in the whitest of cloths but the atmosphere is anything but haughty or ceremonial. Chef Linus Enström (*pictured*) serves hearty European favourites without a concept or a catch in a Fredrik Forsberg-designed interior that centres on an island bar.

The spot was opened by Jonas Wigert in 2016 to replace his former restaurant (and city institution) Bon Bon, which stood the test of time for seven years. However, the successor certainly doesn't suffer at nostalgia's expense. Enström's continental dishes, such as grilled artichoke and burrata, are quite the draw but don't neglect his Scandi crowd-pleasers; our forks are firmly in the gravlax on rye.

9 Kungstensgatan, 114 25
+46 (0)8 248 050
restaurangilse.se

Must-try
Råraka: A mouthwatering dish of sliced, pan-fried potatoes shaped into a pancake and served with whatever your heart desires. Lingonberries are a common topping, as are fried eggs and bacon. Our *råraka* is from PA&Co (*see page 26*) but it's served city-wide.

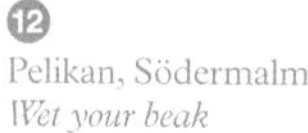

12

Pelikan, Södermalm
Wet your beak

This is the sort of heartwarming restaurant where the waiter has been there for 30 years and the laughter ricochets around the walls until well past bedtime. Pelikan's history goes back to 1664 but it's been serving traditional Swedish fare at this address since 1904.

Don't fill up on the free *knäckebröd*: wait for wholesome plates such as roasted reindeer with root-vegetable terrine and lingonberries. And while the main restaurant may be old-world, there's a more modern bar to the left that serves a mean selection of aquavit.
40 Blekingegatan, 116 62
+46 (0)8 5560 9090
pelikan.se

Must-try
Meatballs at Husmans Deli, Östermalm: A staple that has been served every way possible but is best enjoyed as tradition dictates: at Husmans Deli, fresh from the butcher's, with mashed potatoes, gravy and lingonberries.
husmansdeli.se

13

Portal, Vasastan

Nobel ambition

Chef Klas Lindberg once catered for the Nobel Banquet and chopped away in the kitchen at Alain Passard's L'Arpège in Paris before deciding to strike out on his own. In 2016 he turned a 1960s pub into a restaurant, decked out with Jonas Lindvall chairs and Rosdala pendant lamps, to host his take on Nordic comfort food.

Everyone enjoys the same dishes as the menu is roughly the length of a haiku but it changes every week. The wintry vendace roe, grilled potatoes and egg stew is a tasty affair.

1 St Eriksplan, 113 20
+46 (0)8 301 101
portalrestaurant.se

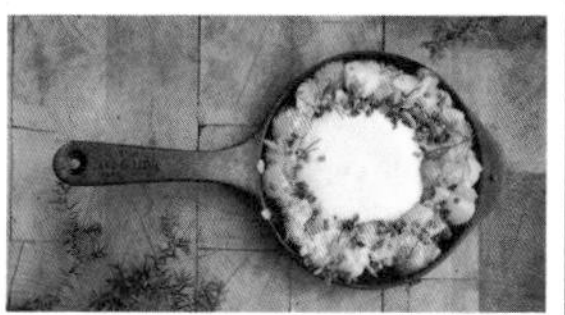

14

Adam/Albin, Vasastan

Raising the bar

Adam Dahlberg and Albin Wessman do fine dining without the red rope or fuss. The young chefs dish out small plates that aren't so small – oxtail ramen, lobster risotto and even fried turbot in flatbread (the "Swedish taco") – in an intimate setting focused around a central marble-top bar. Opt for the latter if space is tight: it's reserved for walk-ins and gains much from the pleasant bustle of the bar and kitchen.

Next door is the duo's casual lunchtime spot Tvätteriet, which feeds the pair's penchant for Japan.

16 Rådmansgatan, 114 25
+46 (0)8 411 5535
adamalbin.se

15

Nytorget 6, Södermalm

Southern belle

When you come to Nytorget 6 the hours seem to pass without you noticing. Open from breakfast until 01.00, this welcoming space is best enjoyed at dusk. The classics are all present but it's the more adventurous plates that have piqued our palates, such as Arctic char on garlic purée or pata negra jamón and goat's cheese tacos.

The dark-wood upstairs is intimate but it's the downstairs, which has a speakeasy charm, where tables are most coveted. On warmer days so is the patio.

6 Nytorget, 116 40
+46 (0)8 640 9655
nytorget6.com

(16)

Woodstockholm, Södermalm
Armchair critic

Furniture designer Johan Edvardsson opened Woodstockholm next door to his showroom and the menu changes every two months, depending on the chef's whim. A recent motif included the recipes of American chef Julia Child, who introduced fine French cooking to the US. The menu is hearty and on the right side of original.

Designer Lars Stensö decided on a white interior but the lighting and furniture are Edvardsson's own. It can all be bought in the showroom, which doubles as a wine bar come summer.
9 Mosebacke torg, 116 46
+46 (0)8 369 399
woodstockholm.com

Lunch
Light bites

1

Barobao, Södermalm
Best buns

Barobao is bright, polished and oh so pretty but it's not the Bumling lamps, blonde-wood furniture or suspended plant pots that have us hooked. The winning formula comes courtesy of Japanese chef Saori Ichihara – formerly of Oaxen (*see page 29*) and Shibumi – who treats well-heeled Södermalmers to lunchtime *bao* (buns). There are several options to choose from but we recommend the fish *tataki* or cauliflower-and-kale variant for the vegetarians.

There are rice boxes too, while the dinner menu is more extensive and offers slower sit-down dishes. Whatever you choose, make sure you snag a bottle of the Yuzu beer. Just don't bother with the glass: serving beer in a jar is the one gimmick that doesn't work in Barobao's favour.
66 Hornsgatan, 118 21
+46 (0)8 643 7776
barobao.com

(2)

Bröderna Svedman, Vasastan
Veggie table

In 2014, brothers Per and Ola Svedman opened something special not far from bustling Odenplan. A few steps down from street level bring you into a simple white-tiled space that hawks exceptional food.

The pair are primarily known for fresh fruit and vegetables but there's also a counter where you can sit and enjoy something delicious – and organic – to eat. The menu is made up of seasonal ingredients that might feature in anything from an artichoke-and-paprika omelette to a salad of roasted vegetables, serrano ham and mozzarella.

On Fridays there's occasionally an "after-work", as the Swedes call it, which includes the serving of beer, charcuterie and sausages to mark the start of the weekend.

54 Dalagatan, 113 25
+46 (0)7 0422 5899
brodernasvedman.se

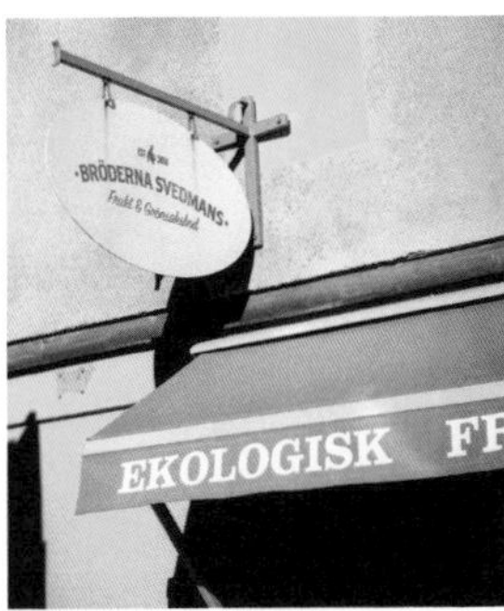

(3)

Broms, Östermalm
Deli delights

Anna Bauer started Broms as a catering business in her cellar in 2006 but when a property developer asked her if she could do something with the ground floor of an old Nordea Bank off Karlaplan, she jumped at the opportunity. The result is a restaurant-cum-deli stocking everything from marmalade and biscuits to cured meat, cheese and still-warm loaves.

The restaurant puts as much care into the menu as its pantry, dishing out generous plates of ox cheek in red wine and seared halibut on a bed of vegetables.

76 Karlavägen, 114 59
+46 (0)8 263 710
bromskarlaplan.se

Three appetising food halls

Stockholm's markets offer everything you'd wish for and more – some even have live music.

01 Hötorgshallen, Norrmalm: There's been an open market on Hötorget Square since about 1640 so it's no wonder that the city formalised the practice with a permanent version here in the 1950s. The choice is extensive and more international than the offering at Östermalms Saluhall (*see page 36*): you'll find everything from mortadella ham to fresh lobster and lychees.
hotorgshallen.se

02 Söderhallarna, Södermalm: A colourful sprawl of fresh produce alongside a score of cafés for those looking to grab a bar-stool bite (try Melanders for fresh seafood). The hall was set up in 1992 and so lacks the old-world charm of its two counterparts. But what it's missing in architectural allure it makes up for in quality.
soderhallarna.se

03 Teatern at Ringen, Södermalm: Across the counter you'll find top-notch chefs offering a casual sample of their cuisine: Adam Dahlberg and Albin Wessman of Adam/Albin (*see page 33*) pour out bowls of ramen, while Michelin-starred Stefano Catenacci of Operakällaren (*see page 30*) serves truffle ravioli and Gotland beets with goat's cheese. There's live music on Saturday nights too.
ringencentrum.se/teatern

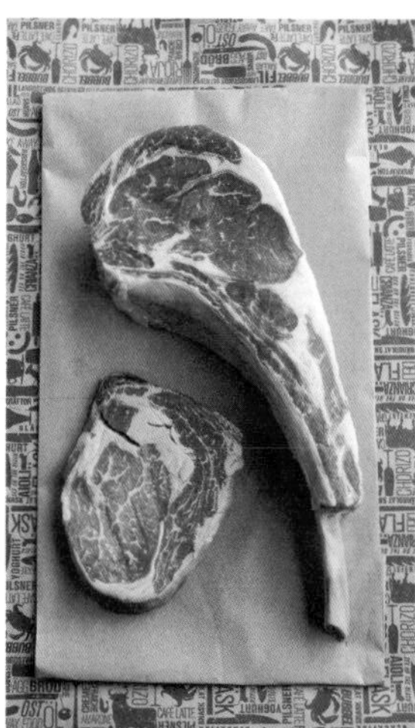

4

Urban Deli, Norrmalm
City pitstop

Despite having a few outposts dotted around the city, each of Urban Deli's shops has a distinct character and always seems full of cheerful souls enjoying languorous lunches. The original spot in Nytorget, Södermalm, is the cosiest of the lot but the newest location in Norrmalm is superb for an afternoon pitstop.

Portions exceed the phrase "generous" and are made with excellent Swedish ingredients, all of which are available from the deli at the front counter; the deep bowls of *fiskgryta*, a seafood casserole, are made with shrimp, mussels and aioli.

The downstairs has a quiet co-working space – if you ignore the keyboard-bashing freelancers – and the roof terrace is a summer spot for alfresco affairs.
44 Sveavägen, 111 34
+46 (0)8 4255 0020
urbandeli.org

5

Östermalms Saluhall, Östermalm
Market value

Ever since it opened in 1888 inside a decorative red-brick building, Östermalms Saluhall has been one of the world's most stunning food markets – not to mention a top Stockholm attraction.

Locals come for the lip-smacking produce, while visitors snap photos and perch for lunch at one of the many counters. And it's made up of resilient retailers: when it closed for a two-year renovation in 2016, all the traders set up shop inside a temporary building on the square across the street.

The starkly modern structure is a great setting for historic merchants, such as butcher Willy Ohlssons and Betsy Sandberg's chocolate shop. It remains one of the best places to shop, lunch or pap a few photos of spirited vendors and tasty takeaways.
Östermalmstorg, 114 39
ostermalmshallen.se

⑥

Taverna Brillo, Östermalm
Multiple choice

A restaurant, deli, flower shop, pizzeria and gelateria huddled around a 150-year-old olive tree. Sounds eclectic but the end result is charming and loses nothing in quality, despite the multiple offerings.

The main restaurant in the Jonas Bohlin-designed space serves Swedish and European dishes until 02.00 but if your time is scarce this spot is also ideal for lunch. Head straight to the pizzeria and ask baker Håkan Johansson for one of his efforts with chanterelles, bacon, lardons and Swedish svecia cheese.
6 Sturegatan, 114 35
+46 (0)8 5197 7800
tavernabrillo.se

⑦

Pom & Flora, Vasastan
Brunch time

A cinnamon bun on the go is a good breakfast but set aside time for a sit-down feast at Pom & Flora. There's a little Södermalm outpost but the larger Vasastan venue wins out, not least because of the Emma Olbers-designed interior that lends it a country-house charm.

The breakfast (owner Anna Axelsson was inspired by the Australian cafés she came across during her travels) is healthy, hearty and organic. It's too tough to call between the colourful chia pudding bowls and homely avocado on rye so opt for the sizeable "weekend brunch" which offers a taste of everything.
39 Odengatan, 113 51
+46 (0)7 6249 6701
pomochflora.se

Dramatic dinner

Teatergrillen in Norrmalm has been frequented by the city's film stars since 1945 (Ingmar Bergman among them). The candle-lit and theatre-like interior by director Yngve Gamlin is paired with exquisite European cuisine by chef Peder Andreasen.
teatergrillen.se

⑧
Lennart & Bror, Vasastan
Chew the fat

Carnivores should pull up a chair at this friendly butcher-cum-deli. Serving a lunch menu of sausages with sauerkraut, steak sandwiches and charcuterie platters to name a few, founders Rasmus Ek and Fritjof Andersson (*both pictured, Ek on right*) offer the best cuts from the city's former meatpacking district.

The school friends joined forces after agreeing that there was a shortage of good butchers. "They haven't been a thing in Sweden for nearly 50 years now. For us it was about having a relationship with the people over the counter."
83 Birger Jarlsgatan, 113 48
+46 (0)7 3420 2053
lennartochbror.se

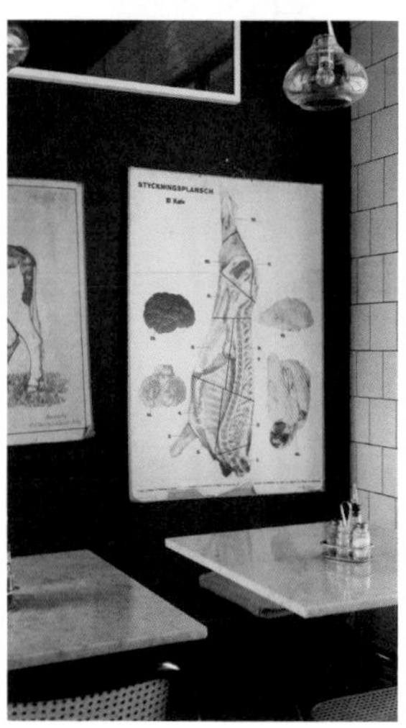

Coffee shops
Enjoy the daily grind

Kaffeverket, Vasastan
Has bean

At Kaffeverket you can take a *fika* break like a true Stockholmer. Since it was founded in 2009, this café has championed coffee and sources the best beans from Brazil and beyond.

It certainly makes a mean Cup of Joe, which locals rave about, but the food and pastries aren't to be overlooked. The counter is laden with a bounty of sweet and savoury treats, all of which are made fresh daily (the pastries direct from the in-house bakery). It's no surprise that this cosy café with its white tiles and grey-wood accents has become an institution.
88 Sankt Eriksgatan, 113 62
+46 (0)8 315 142
kaffeverket.nu

Vete-Katten, Norrmalm
Rising fortunes

Vete-Katten opened in 1928 and drew on the genteel style of its venerated Viennese counterparts. It hasn't always been the sumptuous space it is today: the bakery has grown tenfold over the past century. The secret to its success is, of course, the matchless offering. "We're famous for our princess cake, as well as our Budapest-style pastries," says head pastry chef Johan Sandelin.

There's a separate tearoom at the back if you want to avoid the hustle of the main hall but be prepared to serve yourself.
55 Kungsgatan, 111 22
+46 (0)8 208 405
vetekatten.se

③
Johan & Nyström, Södermalm
Munch bunch

Johan & Nyström is the quintessential hangout for Södermalm's cool cats, opened by a group of coffee-loving Stockholmers in 2008. There's a second branch in Kungsholmen but this larger split-level space is our favourite.

The coffee hails primarily from Brazil, Ethiopia and Indonesia. Beyond a good brew you'll find perhaps the most delectable sandwiches in town: the taleggio, apple and beetroot on rye is a splendid combination. Take your treat down to the cosy stadium-style tiered seating on the lower floor, where you can browse the colourful bags of coffee and Fellow Stagg copper kettles (all for sale) while you eat.

7 Swedenborgsgatan, 118 48
+46 (0)8 702 2040
johanochnystrom.se

④
Café Pascal, Vasastan
Family affair

Pascal is the effort of Arman, Hosep and Jannet Seropian, three siblings from Armenia. Coffee is an integral part of their culture so they named the café after Pascal Harutiun: an Armenian Parisian who opened one of Europe's first coffee shops in 1672.

The superlative brew (there are three slow-drips working at all times) is sourced from Lund-based Love Coffee Roasters; modest but excellent food completes the offering. Few patrons take their coffee to go: the atmosphere is as much an attraction as the black stuff.

4 Norrtullsgatan, 113 29
+46 (0)8 316 110
cafepascal.se

⑤
Drop Coffee, Södermalm
Fab flagship

Drop Coffee is a big player in the international coffee game: its brews – made from Ethiopian and Colombian beans that have been roasted at the company's own roastery on the outskirts of Stockholm – have won a glut of awards.

At its flagship, silky cortados and punchy filter coffees are poured with scientific precision and served to customers perched patiently on tan-coloured stools. The interior is low-key and the food options minimal but with coffee this good, it doesn't matter.

10 Wollmar Yxkullsgatan, 118 50
+46 (0)7 6369 8070
dropcoffee.com

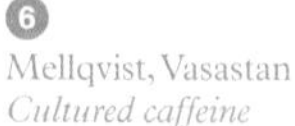

6
Mellqvist, Vasastan
Cultured caffeine

Stockholm is not, alas, brimming with cafés like Paris or Vienna – which makes the one that Erik Mellqvist opened in 1997 all the more extraordinary. From 06.00, locals swing by for great coffee (roasted by David Haugaard, who also supplies King Carl XVI Gustaf) and maybe a breakfast tray with a sandwich, yoghurt and juice.

There are tempting cardamom buns and sourdough baguettes, as well as vegan dishes and lactose and gluten-free soup at lunchtime. It's busy all day long but you can always grab something to go from the stall outside.
4 Rörstrandsgatan, 113 40
+46 (0)8 302 380

7
Il Caffè, Södermalm
Home comforts

This coffee shop in Sofo (South of Folkungagatan) is always packed. Whether it's the cinnamon buns and freshly ground beans that keep people coming back, or the laidback atmosphere and fragrant florist next door, one thing's clear: the combination is a winner. The oven-hot treats, smell of coffee and peonies from Christoffers Blommor (*see page 52*) are hard to resist.

Il Caffè is suited to every occasion, from coffee with friends to business lunches and plugging in with a laptop. And with its homely feel, there's a good chance you'll want to linger.
23 Södermannagatan, 116 40
ilcaffe.se

8
Rosendals Trädgårdkafé, Djurgården
Gardeners' world

The gardens around Rosendal Palace have been cultivated by a community-run foundation since 1982 – and at the centre is a café with simple country charm. A wooden table is piled high with pastries and cakes that go beyond cinnamon buns (think chunky pies with apple and pear), as well as lunch plates that change daily.

You can buy whatever the gardens grow, from pumpkin seeds to apple cider. Plus, if the weather's clement, amble down to the idyllic orchard and maze.
12 Rosendalsterrassen, 115 21
+46 (0)8 5458 1270
rosendalstradgard.se

On the rise

A dozen or so little bakeries by the name of Fabrique are dotted around town and make excellent cinnamon buns, sourdough bread and delectable sandwiches (the bresaola and pesto-butter combination is our pick). Try the sticky walnut bun too.
fabrique.se

Bakeries
Fresh from the oven

① Kafé Konditori Valand, Vasastan
Enduring love

In 1954, Stellan Åström designed and opened a café and hired a young Polish woman to work there. More than six decades later Magdalena (*pictured*), who subsequently became Mrs Åström, still comes in each week to bake an array of traditional Swedish cakes and pastries. She also waits the tables.

Magdalena is now in her eighties but Valand, with its original teak panelling and mid-century furnishings, has barely changed since opening day. The fact that the food is delicious just adds to the appeal of Stockholm's best-preserved mid-century café.
48 Surbrunnsgatan, 113 48
+46 (0)8 300 476

② Robin Delselius, Södermalm
Cult croissants

Bakeries run in the Delselius family's DNA. Robin Delselius's parents founded this small chain of patisseries that you'll spy in neighbouring town Gustavsberg and, in 2016, the young Stockholmer branched out on his own.

This roomy outpost on a Södermalm side-street has charming details, including a lit candle on every marble table. Most importantly, however, it serves flaky, buttery pastries (the croissants are a standout), as well as healthier options such as granola or smoothies.
19 Renstiernas gata, 116 31
+46 (0)8 4080 1615
robindelseliusbageri.se

③
Petrus, Södermalm
French fancies

Petrus and Alexandra Jakobsson's diminutive bakery off Mariatorget is chock full of residents and knowing travellers. But they don't flock here for the cinnamon buns: the pièces de résistance are the pains au chocolat and croissants. And though it may seem odd to eat French pastries in Sweden, you'll be singing a different tune once you taste them.

A rare house speciality is the Kouign-amann from Brittany but it's baked at unpredictable intervals at Petrus's whim, so you'll need a bit of luck in nabbing one.
4B Swedenborgsgatan, 118 48
+46 (0)8 6415 2111

④
Bakery & Spice, Norrmalm
Bread winner

No sandwiches, no coffee, no little tables for folks to sit at: Bakery & Spice is all about the organic sourdough bread that it bakes in a stone oven. There's a bread of the day and a bread of the week; there's crispbread coated in poppyseeds too, as well as cookies and cakes.

Open since 2008 and a pioneer of the sourdough craze that swept through Stockholm, it supplies bread to about 50 hotels and cafés in town but this is its only retail outlet. On a warm day pick up a roll to eat in Vasaparken at the end of the street.
46 Torsgatan, 113 62
+46 (0)8 333 990
bakeryandspice.se

Bars
Raise a glass

1

Bleck, Södermalm
Park it

There are plenty of spots in which to enjoy a summer's evening in Stockholm but few rival Bleck. Sat in the newly opened park Lilla Blecktornsparken, the restaurant-bar's main allure is the rustic terrace; perched under a towering oak tree and softly lit by twinkling fairy lights, it sees Stockholmers clinking glasses until 01.00 on Friday and Saturday.

The menu is light but rich and with a penchant for seafood: octopus served with celeriac and oyster is a speciality. There's also plenty for vegetarians, such as grilled avocado and aubergine on *socca* (a Genovese crêpe). Follow this with a bottle of muscadet or one of the crowd-drawing cocktails. Our pick is the Bittergrape, a hibiscus and lemon-based take on the negroni.
68 Katarina Bangata, 116 42
+46 (0)8 452 9559
restaurangbleck.se

I intend to make natural wine – and drink it, naturally

2

Tyge & Sessil, Östermalm
Top cellar

Tyge & Sessil is buoyant, bustling and just around the corner from Stureplan. In the unpretentious interior, chef Niklas Ekstedt is living out his dream of running an avant garde wine bar not far from his eponymous restaurant (*see page 27*). Offering more than 300 natural wines, this is the place to find one-off sensations from small producers such as France's Domaine Singla in Roussillon. His friend and sommelier, Maximilian Mellfors, has developed a menu to complement the wine and there is a piano for guests to play until 01.00.
4 Brahegatan, 114 37
+46 (0)8 5194 2277
tygesessil.se

3

Folkölsbutiken, Södermalm
Drinking buddies

Friends Johan Palo and Johan Ekfeldt – founder of coffee shop Johan & Nyström (*see page 39*) – have a penchant for beer but found it hard to share their passion due to Swedish law: in Sweden all tipples above 4 per cent are sold through state-owned Systembolaget shops.

So the pair set up a shop selling beer below the 3.5 per cent threshold from small-batch brewers; expect ales, ciders, lagers and pilsners in attractive bottles. We have a soft spot for the Saison d'Être, made by nearby Stockholm Brewing Co.
42A Hornsgatan, 118 21
+46 (0)736 769 949
folkolsbutiken.se

4

Gaston, Gamla Stan
Grape expectations

This is an elegant wine bar on the Old Town waterfront with a cellar that stocks about 400 wines, from France, Germany, Austria, Italy and California. It was opened in 2014 by the Michelin-starred chef Björn Frantzén and has seen a flattering footfall ever since.

Patrons with an aversion to long wine lists ought to try one of the 12 daily-changing bottles chosen by sommelier Janni Berndt, which are best paired with small plates from Frantzén's next-door gastro pub, The Flying Elk.

Once a bottle is done for, Berndt places the cork into the grooved partings of the wooden wall, building a viticultural mosaic – a masterpiece that Stockholmers are particularly keen to flock to (and supplement) come Friday evening.
15 Mälartorget, 111 28
+46 (0)8 4002 0604
gastonvin.se

5

Katarina Ölkafé, Södermalm
Tasteful arrangement

This pint-sized bar stocks an encyclopaedic range of beers from microbreweries across Sweden. The pretty bottles form a library of libations, illuminated by lantern-style lamps. During the winter, well-heeled folk huddle around the taps then spill out onto the street as soon as summer arrives. It's a thrill in all seasons.

Those hunkering down for a long session needn't worry about grumbling stomachs: the kitchen's generously loaded sandwiches draw the crowds as steadily as the drinks.
27 Katarina Bangata, 116 39
+46 (0)8 644 6443
katarinaolkafe.se

Kvarnen, Södermalm

Step back in time

Kvarnen has seen it all during its century-long existence: it served cheap grub to the unemployed in the 1930s; transformed into a Bavarian beer hall in the 1950s; had a stint as a linoleum-decked English pub in the 1960s; and became a hangout for musicians and left-wing politicians in the 1990s.

Today it has reverted to its original 1908 look, with jovial punters perched on the wooden benches for traditional *skagen* toast, or huddling around the brass beer vats. On weekends, Södermalmers often drink here until 03.00.

4 Tjärhovsgatan, 116 21
+46 (0)8 643 0380
kvarnen.com

7

Folii, Södermalm

Wine and dine

Restaurateur Jonas Sandberg and sommelier Béatrice Becher's wine bar offers homely charm and some 250 wines by the glass from France and Italy, not to mention a charcuterie selection that Sandberg tends to as meticulously as the cellar (the prosciutto and taleggio with apple chutney is the star dish).

The duo designed the place in collaboration with Oslo bar Territoriet, on whose look they modelled their own. Seats can be scarce in what's a small space but there are worse things than a glass of wine at the bar with Becher.

21 Erstagatan, 116 36
+46 (0)8 380 048
folii.se

Bar Central, Södermalm

Trendy on tap

Inspiration comes from central Europe at this cool-meets-cosy bar, which is no surprise seeing as Swedish owner Robert Rudinski has a Serbian father, a Hungarian-Croatian mother and a Hungarian crew in the kitchen.

There's Czech pilsner on tap and schnitzel, *spätzle* (German pasta) and pierogi on the menu; the lace curtains and coasters were made by Rudinski's mother-in-law's cousin in Serbia. Among the cluster of hip hangouts surrounding Nytorget, this is easily our favourite.

83 Skånegatan, 116 35
+46 (0)8 644 2420
barcentral.se

Retail
Simple sell

Stockholmers have mastered the art of presentation and as such their city is full of beautiful, albeit often understated, things. Shops more than elsewhere are sleek: clad in concrete, accented with pale wood and manned by smiley attendants.

In Södermalm and Östermalm, classy flagships from Sweden's world-famous fashion labels sit alongside lesser-known shoemakers, plus ateliers touting Swedish-made jewellery and unerringly tasteful Scandinavian homeware.

But Stockholm surprises too. It's home to one of Europe's finest department stores (a rare old-world type that hasn't yet lost its elan to chains). In Gamla Stan, a hole-in-the-wall florist is tucked away down a cobbled street, while quirky record shops stand side by side with peerless magazine purveyors. Here's our take on where to fill your bags with the best from the capital's burgeoning shopping scene.

Homeware
House style

① Dusty Deco, Östermalm
Vintage find

Edin Memic Kjellvertz (*pictured*) started collecting furniture on his travels while working for Acne Studios (*see page 58*). When his stockpile grew so large that it could no longer be contained in his apartment, he and his wife Lina opened Dusty Deco.

In 2017 they opened another space in Östermalm, where 1970s lamps from Murano heavyweight Venini sit next to upholstered ottomans by US designer Jonathan Adler. The outside looks more like a florist than a furniture shop but duck inside to uncover the booty.
21 Brahegatan, 114 37
+46 (0)8 5449 9195
dustydeco.com

②

Nordiska Galleriet, Norrmalm

Magnificent multibrand

Nordiska Galleriet's products stretch over three floors and include everything from Skultuna brass bowls and David Chipperfield lamps to wooden toys by the late Danish designer Kay Bojesen.

The shop has been here since 1912 and can count among its merits the early adoption of pieces by modernists, including Arne Jacobsen; it also backs talents such as the fledgling Brooklyn lighting brand Roll & Hill. Its latest innovation is the NG1912 Studio: an in-house interiors consultancy for shoppers.

11 Nybrogatan, 114 39
+46 (0)8 442 8360
nordiskagalleriet.se

③

Svenskt Tenn, Östermalm

Colourful context

Art teacher Estrid Ericson invested her inheritance in a modest pewter business known as Svenskt Tenn in 1924 but it was only when she collaborated with Viennese architect and designer Josef Frank (*see page 91*) that she cracked the market. The vivacious palette used here is a floral pick-me-up in a city known for its minimalism; 80 per cent of the shop's colourful cushions, florid tableware and cheerful furniture is based on original designs (Frank left behind some 2,000 sketches and ideas).

Among the spread on offer you'll find a range from contemporary designers such as Per Öberg and Sigurd Persson. If you're just browsing you can enjoy the exhibitions that are often staged on the ground floor, or take a break in the upstairs tearoom.

5 Strandvägen, 114 51
+46 (0)8 670 1600
svenskttenn.se

Mid-century furniture designers

Scandinavian design has taken over living rooms around the world but there's far more to Sweden's canon than Ikea.

01 Greta Magnusson-Grossman (1906-1999): Her iconic cone-head and tripod-base Grasshopper lamp has been much-aped since its release in 1947.

02 Carl Malmsten (1888-1972): His wooden Lilla Åland chair is one of the quintessential expressions of the 1920s Swedish grace design movement.

03 Bruno Mathsson (1907-1988): Mathsson brought a rustic look to Stockholm's living rooms. His Eva chair features a beech frame covered with plaited linen.

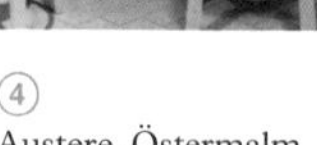

④

Austere, Östermalm
Fully furnished

Behind an unassuming door on pedestrianised Nybrogatan, this space is austere by name but inviting in execution. The parquet flooring and blue walls set a tasteful tone for the fine furniture within.

The goodies include Richard Palmquist ceramics, the W171 Alma pendant by Wästberg and angular Arrow tables from founder Fredrik Carlström and designer Erik Järkil. Behind the shop is a coffee counter and behind that is Alma, Stockholm's best co-working-cum-members space, the work of architecture firm Tham & Videgård.

8 Nybrogatan, 114 34
+1 (844) 287 8373
austere.co

⑤

E Torndahl, Gamla Stan
Woman's touch

With gold shopfront lettering, a gilded ceiling and a creaky wooden floor there are ample indications that this shop has been in business for yonks. Founded in 1864 by Ida Thekla Sabina Kunigunda Thorndahl, it has been passed down to the women in the family; today it is run by her great-great-granddaughter Lotta Imberg.

Now, as then, the focus is on excellent Scandinavian design: bags by Sandqvist and Hay stationery sit alongside cheeky children's clothes by Mini Rodini and cheery illustrated posters by OMM Design.

63 Västerlånggatan, 111 29
+46 (0)8 103 409
etorndahl.se

⑥

Kaolin, Södermalm
License to kiln

Kaolin has displayed tableware and ornaments by Swedish ceramicists since 1978 and today presents wares by more than 20 artists – mostly Stockholmers – who take it in turns to man the counter.

"I've been part of Kaolin for 15 years: it's a great place to showcase new work and meet people interested in ceramics," says sculptor Eva Larsson, whose bronze figures stand alongside Lars Bergstrom striped cups and teapots by Ann-Sofie Gelfius. A gallery space at the front hosts a new exhibition every month.

50 Hornsgatan, 118 21
+46 (0)8 644 4600
kaolin.se

7
Asplund, Östermalm
Simply Swedish

When siblings Michael and Thomas Asplund founded this shop in 1990, they conceptualised it as a gallery that displayed furniture as works of art (which makes sense given Michael's former career as an art dealer). The stripped-back space was designed by architects Claesson Koivisto Rune to echo the minimalistic nature of the objects on display.

Everything is created in collaboration with local designers, from wooden cabinets by Broberg & Ridderstråle to Thomas Sandell's award-winning metal Air bench.
31 Sibyllegatan, 114 42
+46 (0)8 665 7360
asplund.org

8
Props by Kampmann, Östermalm
Theatrical affair

Opened in 2016, this shop, office and gallery hybrid from interior stylist Annika Kampmann (*pictured*) has all the hallmarks of her skills as a visual merchandiser for Ralph Lauren and Max Mara, plus a hint of her stylist's eye for winsome homeware. Think Malmö-made rugs, Emil Kjellberg vases, plates from Studio EK and a marble-bottomed mirror made with designer Petra Lilja.

The goods sit towards the avant garde end of the spectrum but Kampmann certainly deserves props for her originality.
24 Grevgatan, 114 53
+46 (0)73 390 3096
propsbykampmann.com

⑨
Perspective Studio, Vasastan
Eclectic selection

Opposite a bustling intersection, Robin Klang and Ejub Bicic have built a space that is quite unlike Stockholm's other furniture spots. Mirrored surfaces – whether low coffee tables or high pedestals – provide a striking contrast to the chalky-textured paint on the walls.

Klang previously worked as a fashion buyer and his expertise is evident in the eclectic selection on show here, which includes 160-year-old Chinese chairs and pottery and leather products from students at Stockholm's Konstfack art school.

15 Sankt Eriksplan, 113 20
+46 (0)7 0729 7956
perspectivestudio.se

Specialist retailers
Areas of expertise

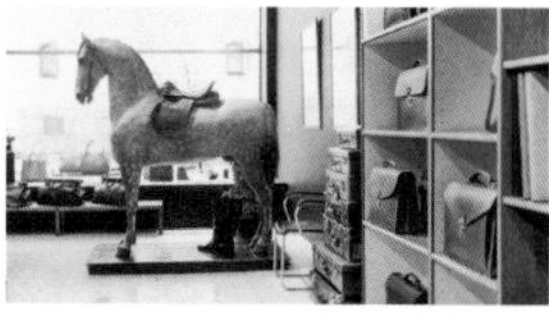

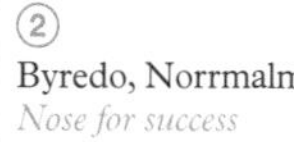

①
Palmgrens, Östermalm
Swell for leather

This brand's heritage harks back to 1896 when Johannes Palmgrens began fashioning saddles and other riding equipment at the very same address. In fact the wooden horse on which he tested his creations still sits at the back of the shop.

Today the label focuses on smaller leather goods such as briefcases, wallets and handbags, made of vegetable-tanned leather in vivid colours. Its mesh-front rattan bag, made from interlaced palm, is a Stockholm favourite, inspired by the fashionable wicker bags worn in southern Europe in the 1950s.

7 Sibyllegatan, 114 51
+46 (0)8 667 9040
palmgrens.se

②
Byredo, Norrmalm
Nose for success

Byredo founder Ben Gorham isn't your typical perfumer. The Canadian-Indian was raised in Stockholm and embarked on a pro-basketball career before deciding that he would rather concoct fragrances than shoot hoops. He launched his first fragrance in 2006 and today his scents are stocked in the world's finest shops.

At its flagship, glass shelves are laden with body lotions and hand creams, as well as hundreds of black-capped bottles filled with sweet aromas. Our pick is the rose-scented Blanche.

6 Mäster Samuelsgatan, 111 44
+46 (0)8 5250 2615
byredo.com

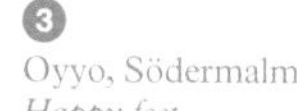

3

Oyyo, Södermalm
Happy feet

"Growing up in Sweden, flat-weave rugs were an inherent part of our homes," says Marcus Åhrén, who co-founded this textiles studio with Lina Zedig (*both pictured*). The duo's cheery *dhurries* (traditional Indian flat-weaves) are handmade in a workshop in rural Maharashtra. "They are a tribute to a dying craft," says Åhrén of the organic-cotton rugs, which are brightened up with plant-based dyes.

All are displayed – whether hung from white walls or rolled across sand-coloured tables – in a light-filled showroom that can be visited by appointment.
94 Brännkyrkagatan, 117 26
oyyo.se

④

La Bruket, Södermalm

Save your skin

Irritated by the quality of skincare products on the market, Monica Kylén (*pictured*) decided to make her own. There's a Swedish bent to the goods, which are inspired by the spa tradition of Vårberg where Kylén grew up, and where salt and seaweed are used for skin ailments.

Everything is made from organic ingredients: salt scrubs with eucalyptus, rosemary hand creams and lip balms made of beeswax and almond oil. Try them at the striking flagship, designed by art director James Brooks; its wave-like walls are a nod to the brand's coastal roots.

19 Södermannagatan, 116 40
+46 (0)8 615 0011
labruket.se

⑤

Christoffers Blommor, Gamla Stan

Blooming marvellous

This charming building in Gamla Stan has been home to florists since the 1960s, with affable Stockholmer Christoffer Broman (*pictured*) taking over in 2001.

Ivy has a strong showing outside, while inside seasonal plants – including white tulips and yellow acacias – engulf the small space. Most are sourced in Årsta, south of Stockholm, and include varieties from South Africa, Ecuador, Denmark and Italy. "We follow the seasons and always prefer wild bouquets that look like you have picked them yourself," says Broman.

10 Kåkbrinken, 111 27
+46 (0)8 240 075
christoffersblommor.se

⑥

Skultuna, Östermalm

Bold as brass

Brass is starting to feel like the modish metal for inspiration-lacking designers but Skultuna's showroom is a reminder that well-made products outlast the fads.

Skultuna has been around since 1607 but wears its legacy lightly. The highlights of its homeware range include contemporary-looking vases and tea-light holders, while cufflinks, bangles and bracelets make perfect gifts. The brand is a favourite with the design cognoscenti and can be seen everywhere from the pages of glossy magazines to the Royal Palace.

18 Grev Turegatan, 114 46
+46 (0)8 5458 3555
skultuna.com

7

Triwa, Östermalm
Timely endeavour

In 2007, four friends banded together to create a range of Stockholm-made timepieces with leather straps from Swedish tannery Tärnsjö Garveri. Their pink Elding Oscarson-designed shop opened in 2014 and also stocks the brand's built-to-last sunglasses.

"We ran pop-ups in different locations in Stockholm before we opened here," says CEO and co-founder Harald Wachtmeister. "The space is small and ideal for our watches and accessories." True enough: business has been ticking along nicely ever since.
13 Grev Turegatan, 114 46
+46 (0)70 140 8957
triwa.com

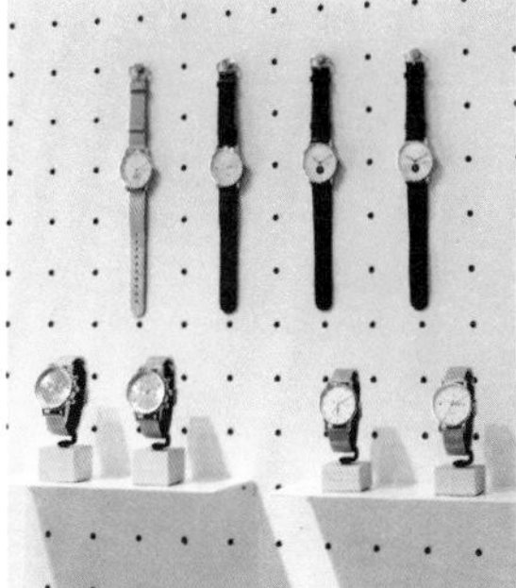

Menswear
Sartorial essentials

1

Saman Amel, Östermalm
Keeping it simple

This atelier doesn't look like your average tailor. Inside a white room its founders Saman Amel and Dag Granath (*both pictured, Granath on left*) are surrounded by grey double-breasted blazers and crisp white shirts. "We want to present something that is different from other tailors," says Granath. "Our Scandinavian heritage is prevalent in the muted tones."

Their pieces are handmade in Italy, with tweaks in Stockholm. Granath believes that less is more: "We don't want to make the outfit scream for attention."
21 Kommendörsgatan, 114 48
+46 (0)7 6199 7086
samanamel.se

② Uniforms for the Dedicated, Södermalm
Sustainable threads

Founded in 2008, this shop is all about sustainability: everything from tailoring to streetwear is assembled from organic, bio-based or recycled fabrics. Its latest designs, such as jersey-cotton suit jackets, corduroy trousers and linen T-shirts, can be picked up at its flagship, which opened in 2012.

Formerly a post office, the white-walled space mimics the clothes' clean lines and handsome looks. "We built the shop ourselves using upcycled materials such as timber," says co-founder Lars Hedberg.
24 Krukmakargatan, 118 51
+46 (0)8 5333 2448
uniformsforthededicated.com

Best street

Krukmakargatan is our favourite shopping strip, a claim backed up by having the remarkable print specialist Papercut sandwiched between top fashion outposts Nitty Gritty, Uniforms For The Dedicated and Our Legacy.

③ Our Legacy, Södermalm
Dapper duds

In this concrete-clad shop, suede bomber jackets hang alongside 1990s-style corduroy trousers. More than a decade since Stockholmers Jockum Hallin and Christopher Nying created a line of T-shirts, their label has blossomed into one of Scandinavia's hippest menswear brands.

Its pieces now run the gamut from trainers to sunglasses. The original shop has been joined by a roomier space in Norrmalm and an archive shop in Vasastan, where you can snap up discounted gems from the past decade.
24-26 Krukmakargatan, 118 51
+46 (0)8 668 2060
ourlegacy.se

④ Skoaktiebolaget, Östermalm
Best foot forward

Patrik Löf (*pictured*) and his partner Daniel Tung opened this shop in 2012, specialising in handmade shoes from smaller Swedish manufacturers. "Our shoes are three or four times more expensive than most but they will last for 25 years and are made by small, often family-owned factories in Europe," says Löf.

Other brands include Italy's Enzo Bonafé and UK staple John Lobb. Stockholm firm Broberg & Ridderstråle designed the space like a luxurious walk-in-closet, with warm wooden finishes.
23 Nybrogatan, 114 39
+46 (0)8 6840 9684
skoaktiebolaget.se

⑤
AW Bauer & Co, Norrmalm
Bespoke suiting

"Our cut is Scandinavian, not Milanese as some assume," says Frederik Andersen, who co-owns 150-year-old AW Bauer & Co with four fellow tailors. Its suits are stitched in a glass-walled studio at the back of the shop, a standard two-piece lounge suit taking two to three months to assemble.

If you don't have time to wait, browse the silk hankies and fleur-de-lis cufflinks newly added to the in-house range, or Andersen's perfume collaboration with Byredo (*see page 50*): Ombra delle 5.
4 Brunnsgatan, 111 38
+46 (0)8 104 780
awbauer.com

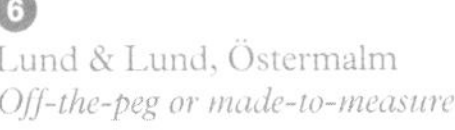

6
Lund & Lund, Östermalm
Off-the-peg or made-to-measure

Lund & Lund has been kitting out Stockholm's chaps since 1963, when brothers Hans and Jesper Lund returned to the city after learning pattern-cutting in New York and London. Today their shop has retained its old-school charm: blazers from Tokyo's Ring Jacket and a host of Italian labels such as Caruso hang in dark-wood closets, while suede trainers from Sweden's CQP are lined up in front of tan-leather armchairs.

The shop also offers made-to-measure suit tailoring, so you can select your own cloth and lining.
12 Sturegatan, 114 36
+46 (0)8 661 0735
lundochlund.se

⑦
Second Sunrise, Södermalm
Good jeans

"We have been passionate about denim for a long time and, before opening the shop, we were making jeans in our basement," says Douglas Luhanko, who founded Second Sunrise with his brother Hampus. This workwear shop and repair studio possesses style and grit in equal measure.

The brothers' jeans sit alongside US labels Lee and Filson, as well as hard-to-find Swedish brands that fit the heritage feel. "We carry clothes with classic cuts that are made to last: we enjoy finding pieces that are as usable today as they would have been in the 1940s," says Douglas.
69 Katarina Bangata, 116 42

Snappy shirts

Founded in 2012 by a trio of self-confessed shirt nerds, Schnayderman's understated designs have quickly made their way into menswear shops around the world. If you're in town for the weekend visit its flagship, open Saturdays only.
schnaydermans.com

Womenswear
Ladies first

Plain simple

Rodebjer's interior is all about clean lines

② Caroline Hjerpe, Södermalm
Precious things

Caroline Hjerpe has come a long way since teaching herself to make rings by watching online videos. The Stockholm native wanted to be a therapist but hasn't looked back since launching her women's jewellery label in 2014.

"I'm so much happier now than I would ever be somewhere else," says Hjerpe, who hand-makes all the wares at her shop. In the light-filled space, delicate gold bangles and vintage-style rings with rose-cut diamonds are displayed alongside stationery from Swedish illustrators such as Matilda Svensson and Sonia Cavallini.

132 Åsögatan, 116 24
carolinehjerpe.se

① Rodebjer, Norrmalm
Style you can bank on

Elegant dresses and coats are the hallmarks of this brand, founded by Swede Carin Rodebjer while in New York in the late 1990s. Its flagship, once a bank, smacks of an art gallery, and is almost as striking as the designs within.

"I was really intrigued by the idea of turning this old bank into a palace for women," says Rodebjer. "I wanted to mix earthy elements with a dash of Italian design." Look out for the curved iron sconce lights and the enormous box-like terracotta front desk.

12 Smålandsgatan, 111 46
+46 (0)8 611 0117
rodebjer.com

3

Keen, Vasastan
Fashion frontrunner

Despite its abundance of top fashion labels, Stockholm is somewhat lacking in excellent multibrand shops for women. Fortunately Keen is here to show others the way. "We sell stuff that we like to wear," says Michaela Wallerström, who founded the shop in 2006 in a former launderette before transferring it to its current spot, also in Vasastan, in 2016.

Today Wallerström runs the shop with Ninnie Lahnborg and together the duo stock clothing, eyewear and jewellery by Scandinavian designers such as Rodebjer, Hope and Tom Wood, as well as labels from further afield, including Margiela and Black Crane. Guarded by Wallerström's pint-sized affenpinscher Bibi, and kitted out with wooden and black concrete floors and a monochrome palette, Keen is an elegant – and much-needed – presence in the city.
36 Upplandsgatan, 113 28
+46 (0)8 323 373
keenstockholm.se

Jewellery

01 **All Blues:** Fredrik Nathorst and Jacob Skragge's unisex line is handmade from sterling silver and 18-carat gold at an old Stockholm foundry, and can be perused at Keen, Perspective Studio or NK.
allblues.se

02 **Sofia Eriksson:** Eriksson's assortment of chunky gold-plated rings, hoop earrings and geometric silver bangles is handmade in her Stockholm studio and sold at Nitty Gritty.
sofiaerikssonjewelry.com

03 **Cornelia Webb:** Cornelia Webb's pieces include brass earrings and crinkled silver cuffs. Find them at Nitty Gritty or commission a bespoke design.
corneliawebb.com

Mixed
All together now

1

Appletrees, Norrmalm
Shirt shrift

After stints with Swedish denim maestro Isko, Charles Murray moved into shirts with the launch of Appletrees. Along with co-founder Victor Sandberg, what started with a one-off white shirt soon grew to include a vast wardrobe of wares.

All the shirts are made from Egyptian cotton outside Milan. Cuts range from classic button-down to knee-length but the brand's take on patterns is conservative, preferring deep, solid colours. The shop also stocks accessories, including Mulberry silk scarves and Japanese selvedge denim jeans.
29 Artillerigatan, 111 45
appletrees.se

② Acne Studios, Norrmalm
Swedish style spot

In 1973 a Stockholm bank was the scene of a hostage crisis and the birthplace of the term Stockholm Syndrome. Today the building is home to Acne Studios, Sweden's most important fashion label.

The bank's safes have been replaced by rails of clothes – chunky knits, bright sweatshirts and experimental high-fashion pieces – amid the original, ornate marble columns. The vibe of the brand, founded by Jonny Johansson in 1996, is cool enough to rival the chicest houses in Paris, London and Milan.
2 Norrmalmstorg, 111 46
+46 (0)8 8611 6411
acnestudios.com

Golden oldies

If you're a fashion devotee it's also worth paying a visit to the Acne Archive, a no-fuss space in Vasastan. There you can hunt around for and pick up a one-off gem from past Acne collections.
acnearchive.com

③ Gabucci, Östermalm
Roman holiday

Nearly 20 years after opening a menswear shop, Bob Tavakoli (*pictured*) moved it to its current spot in Östermalm in 2013, before adding a womenswear shop a few doors down. The men's offerings are laidback, with Brunello Cucinelli trainers, Incotex trousers and shirts by Neapolitan maker Finamore. Gabucci Donna, the women's outpost, is also an Italian love affair, stocking the likes of Aspesi, Boglioli and Altea.
Men's: 14 Nybrogatan, 114 39
+49 (0)8 678 0730
gabucci.se
Women's: 26 Nybrogatan, 114 39
+49 (0)8 678 0731
gabuccidonna.com

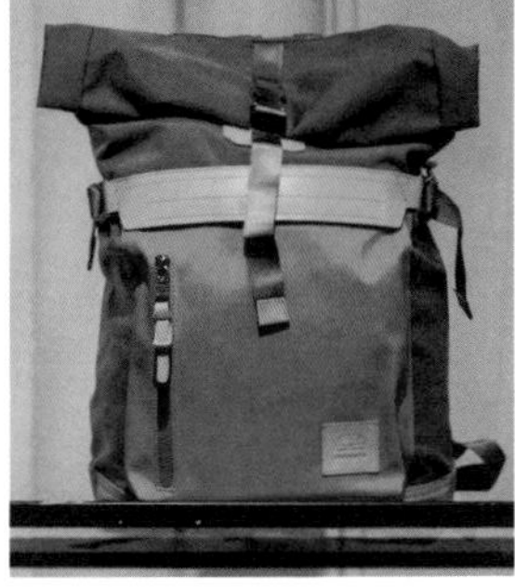

④
Stutterheim, Södermalm
Rain man

Alexander Stutterheim made a splash in 2010 when he injected the humble raincoat with Swedish elegance. Now the former copywriter's waterproofs sell at shops across the city (including Gamla Stan's Designfirman, which makes a significant contribution).

For the full experience head to the flagship, a split-level space accented with hits of colour, from the pink legs of glass display tables to the burgundy, yellow or olive-green "Made in Poland" raincoats that hang oh-so-handsomely around its perimeter.
136 Åsögatan, 116 24
+46 (0)8 4081 0398
stutterheim.com

Sandqvist, Södermalm
Understated charm

Sandqvist, the Stockholm brand that helped pioneer the popularity of backpacks, certainly knows how to make an entrance. When you open the door you're met with a concrete staircase that spirals downwards into the bowels of the building, where the brand's understated look is on full show.

There are signature navy numbers with leather straps, khaki canvas weekenders and smart tan briefcases. Plenty of bag brands now peddle a cool Scandi look but Anton Sandqvist was the first – and remains the finest.
3 Swedenborgsgatan, 118 48
+46 (0)7 6221 0475
sandqvist.net

Swedish trainers

01 **CQP:** These trainers, which are designed in Stockholm and handmade in Portugal, come in dusty shades of suede and are renowned for their arch support (comfy and wearable rather than sore and tricky). You can find them at many of the city's best retailers (including Lund & Lund and Appletrees) or at the brand's flagship on Östermalm's Skeppargatan.
c-qp.com

02 **Spalwart:** From their Stockholm studio, Christoffer Brattin and Fredrik Johansson design retro-looking footwear: think track-style shoes with rubber spikes or chocolate-brown canvas high-tops. Many of their designs are produced in an old factory in Slovakia and they're sold at retailers such as Nitty Gritty (*see page 60*).
spalwart.com

03 **Axel Arigato:** The baby of Gothenburg duo Max Svärdh and Albin Johansson, Axel Arigato makes pared-down trainers with distinctive Margom-rubber platform soles.
axelarigato.com

Tight knit

Alexander Stutterheim's latest venture is a knitwear label called John Sterner. The designer has bought a farm on the island of Öland, where he breeds the sheep whose wool is turned into chunky turtlenecks, cardigans and scarves.
johnsterner.com

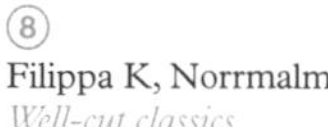

Filippa K, Norrmalm

Well-cut classics

Filippa K's tale began in 1993 when Stockholmer Filippa Knutsson, whose father ran a successful chain of fashion shops, created a collection of first-rate women's basics (an equally wearable menswear line was added four years later). Today Knutsson's products can be found in more than 500 retailers worldwide.

The global flagship is split in two: the women's half is filled with striped shirts, wool trousers and suede boots; the men's side has similarly well-cut pieces, from crew-neck jumpers to leather derbies.

2 Biblioteksgatan, 111 46
+46 (0)8 615 7057
filippa-k.com

Nitty Gritty, Södermalm

His and hers

Nitty Gritty has two spaces a few doors apart, one for men and the other for women. On the men's side sit seasonal items that include striped sweatshirts from The Gigi and retro-style trainers by Spalwart (*see page 59*). For the ladies there are slouchy dresses by Base Range and jewellery from Swedish designers such as Sofia Eriksson.

"Our focus is always to stay relevant," says owner Marcus Söderlind. "We want every brand to serve a purpose here – we don't just want to collect them."

24 and 26 Krukmakargatan, 118 51
+46 (0)8 658 2441 (women's);
+46 (0)8 658 2440 (men's)
nittygrittystore.com

Nudie Jeans Repair Shop, Norrmalm

Jean genies

With their slim cuts, orange stitching and copper buttons, Nudie jeans have become a household name. The label specialises in raw denim and has two locations in the Swedish capital; we suggest the newer one on Jakobsbergsgatan.

The green-walled space feels more workshop than retailer, with staff conducting repairs using old-style sewing machines. You can also pick up new Italian-made jeans here, be they figure-hugging Grim Tims or looser-fitting Steady Eddies.

11 Jakobsbergsgatan, 111 44
+46 (0)10 151 5720
nudiejeans.com

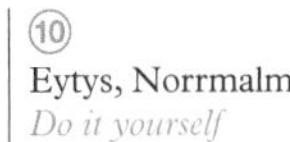

9

NK Department Store, Norrmalm
A different era

Nordiska Kompaniet (NK) is a classy counterpoint to the glut of department stores around the world that have been gutted and filled with generic interiors. Josef Sachs opened the original NK outpost, Sweden's first department store, in Gothenburg in 1864; its Stockholm sibling – an ornate, art nouveau structure – followed in 1915.

Today, as then, it recalls old-world luxury with black-and-white signage, gilded banisters and a magnificent central atrium complete with an arched glass ceiling. Its six marbled storeys showcase everything from flowers to tableware and books (the sprawling fourth-floor bookshop boasts an excellent English-language spread).

Keep an eye out for Paul & Friends on the second level: one of the best menswear spots in the city, this shop-in-shop stocks homegrown labels such as Spalwart and Stutterheim (*see page 59*) alongside international names including Aspesi and Barena.
18-20 Hamngatan, 111 47
+46 (0)8 762 8000
nk.se/stockholm

10

Eytys, Norrmalm
Do it yourself

"I'd been looking for trainers with proportions similar to US navy deck shoes from the 1940s but I couldn't find anything so I started sketching my own," says Max Schiller, who founded Eytys with friend Jonathan Hirschfeld in 2013.

Their brand has made bold strides onto the global scene and the flagship shop is a showstopper. Stockholm designer Axel Wannberg has created a space that nods to both brutalist architecture and Japanese sculptor Shiro Kuramata, with trainers stacked on concrete plinths or along green-tinted glass shelves.
22 Norrlandsgatan, 111 43
+46 (0)8 6844 2080
eytys.com

Concept
Bright ideas

①
Dry Things, Vasastan
Design delights

After years of collaboration, Jenny Tavassoli and Johan Fredlund started Dry Creative Projects design studio. Besides creating visuals for the likes of US fashion house Gant, the duo also beavered away on a line of products that became Dry Things back in 2012.

The shop is stuffed with in-house designed books, graphic prints and wooden chopping boards. The pleasant scattering also includes a line of unisex non-seasonal T-shirts and jackets that are hand-stitched near Bologna in Italy.

36 Upplandsgatan, 113 28
+46 (0)8 218 800
drythings.com

2
Grandpa, Södermalm
Relatively smart

If this shop really was a grandfather it would be more Mick Jagger than moany pensioner. The multi-brand space has two other spots in Stockholm, plus one in Gothenburg, but this is the dapper patriarch of the bunch.

The ground floor stocks Rains coats, Brixtol jackets and Our Legacy shirts, plus blankets from Swedish firm Low Key, T-shirts from AO CMS and comfy own-brand socks and scarves. There are also brass planters from H Skjalm P and soaps from Tangent GC – oh, and books from our own stable.

21 Södermannagatan, 116 40
+46 (0)8 643 6080
grandpa.se

3
Adisgladis, Södermalm
Great outdoors

"I realised I was jealous of the shop owners I was visiting," says Adam Forslund (*pictured*), who opened his own shop after a stint in marketing. The result is outdoor-kit specialist Adisgladis, built by Forslund and his father in 2011.

The place has the whiff of an upmarket hardware shop. Leather trainers from Veja sit on natty plastic shelves, while Kings of Indigo shirts and underwear from The White Briefs dangle from copper hangers. There are also flat-pack barbecues, stainless-steel lanterns and bright thermos flasks.

8 Wollmar Yxkullsgatan, 118 50
+46 (0)7 0968 9362
adisgladis.se

Books and records
Mixed media

1

Papercut, Södermalm
Page boys

Andreas Fryklund and Alexander Dahlberg are unabashed in their pushing of print. Both had run shops for nearly a decade (Fryklund an independent bookshop that also sold films, Dahlberg one of the country's biggest magazine retailers) before they joined forces and opened Papercut together in 2008.

There's nothing about this retailer that says Scandi minimalism: every last inch of the sprawling, fuss-free space has been filled with magazines, books and DVDs. The magazine spread is particularly striking, featuring more than 100 international titles on everything from architecture to cycling and – ahem – erotica.

"Since we've both been in the business for so many years we usually go on our gut feeling," says Fryklund. "'Eclectic' might be the best word to describe our selection: there's something for everyone, from kids to grandpa and grandma."

24-26 Krukmakargatan, 118 51
+46 (0)8 133 574
papercutshop.se

2

Stockholms Fotoantikvariat, Södermalm
Picture books

After years as a teacher, Karl-Erik Jagare opened this shrine to the photographic arts in 2005. The simple space holds new and secondhand books but Jagare excels at first editions that are now out of print. His shop also hosts exhibitions and sells prints.

Over the years its walls have been decorated by works from Gunnar Smoliansky, Catharina Gotby and Tuija Lindström. "I've featured some of Scandinavia's most important photographers," Jagare says without pretence.

31 Torkel Knutssonsgatan, 118 49
+46 (0)8 669 3757
fotoantikvariat.se

③

Rönnells Antikvariat, Norrmalm

Old-time tomes

Rönnells' bright signage and arched entrance are a worthy introduction to one of the country's largest antique bookshops. A fine English-language selection and specialised titles on everything from art to architecture abound – but the real gems are to be found at the back.

Rönnells' rarities span several centuries and include titles unlikely to be found elsewhere (oddly for a Swedish shop, its clutch of first editions by Dickens is renowned). If you're after something elusive, the learned staff will happily help you track it down.

32B Birger Jarlsgatan, 114 29
+46 (0)8 5450 1560
ronnells.se

Konst-ig Books, Södermalm

Masses of volumes

Owners Charlotte Ekbom (*pictured*) and Helene Boström have put together a selection of art, architecture, fashion and photography books that's well worth a leaf through. Their shop started downtown in 1994 but moved here in 2009; its interior is all white, with a concrete floor and a hushed-library vibe.

The packed display tables and shelves hold all manner of printed ephemera, including editions by Swedish imprint Orosdi Back, notebooks from Leuchtturm and limited-edition prints from Swedish photographers.

124 Åsögatan, 116 24
konstigbooks.com

⑤

Pet Sounds Bar, Södermalm

Spin doctors

Pet Sounds opened in 1979 and is proof that music-streaming has yet to topple the record shop. "Södermalm is the best for small shops that are run by their owners; you have lots of regular customers," says Stefan Jacobson, who founded the shop to import records from the UK and US.

Jacobson designed the space himself (with some help from staff, he concedes) and that seems to have involved buying any and all the vinyl he could get his hands on. It's a simple and seductive ensemble that's music to our ears.

53 Skånegatan, 116 37
+46 (0)8 702 9798
psb.bar

Things we'd buy

— Stockholm take-homes

There's a reason that Swedish design is held up and pawed over around the world. Products have a certain sensibility – a sense of style and trend-skipping permanence – and the capital has a predictably promising spread. Envelope-pushing boutiques brim with sharp clothing and careful craftsmanship, as well as Stockholm-made ceramics and watches you can count on and cushions that will cosy-up the most austere-looking living room.

We've waived the tourist tat and looked beyond the souvenir shops for a few well-made products for all seasons: woolly winter socks and a pair of fetching swimmers for a head-first embrace of the archipelago's cool waters come summer.

01 Vika Bröd knäckebröd from Ica *ica.se*
02 *Knacka på!* by Anna-Clara Tidholm (Alfabeta) and *Sakboken* by Stina Wirsén (Rabén & Sjögren), both from Söderbokhandeln *soderbokhandeln.blogspot.com*
03 Brushes, soap dish and shaving cup by Iris Hantverk *irishantverk.se*
04 Birgitta Watz ceramics from Ett Hem *etthem.se*
05 Coffee beans by Drop Coffee *dropcoffee.com*
06 Abba anchovies from Urban Deli *urbandeli.org*
07 Mint chocolate by Urban Deli *urbandeli.org*
08 Salt liquorice by Pärlans *parlanskonfektyr.se*
09 Cederroth moisturising oil from Ica *ica.se*
10 Solstickan matches from Ica *ica.se*
11 Chocolate spread by Pärlans *parlanskonfektyr.se*
12 Kersh Kafferosteri tea from Urban Deli *urbandeli.org*
13 Tea by The Tea Centre of Stockholm *theteacentre.se*
14 Dykes Brewery ale, Närke Kulturbryggeri stout and Eskilstuna Ölkultur IPA, all from Folkölsbutiken *folkolsbutiken.se*
15 Leather laptop case by Palmgrens *palmgrens.se*
16 Stockholms Bränneri gin from Systembolaget *systembolaget.se*
17 See by Us glasses from Stureoptikern *stureoptikern.se*
18 Sunglasses by Triwa *triwa.com*
19 Sunglasses by Vasuma *vasuma.com*
20 Shirts by Our Legacy *ourlegacy.se*
21 Handwash by Björk & Berries *bjorkandberries.com*
22 Teenage Engineering pocket synthesiser from Eye Shut Island *eyeshutisland.com*
23 *Allborgarrätten* by Jan Rydén (Arvinius) from Färgfabriken *fargfabriken.se*
24 Fragrances by Byredo *byredo.com*
25 Nils Olsson Dala horse from Little Sweden *14 Västerlånggatan*

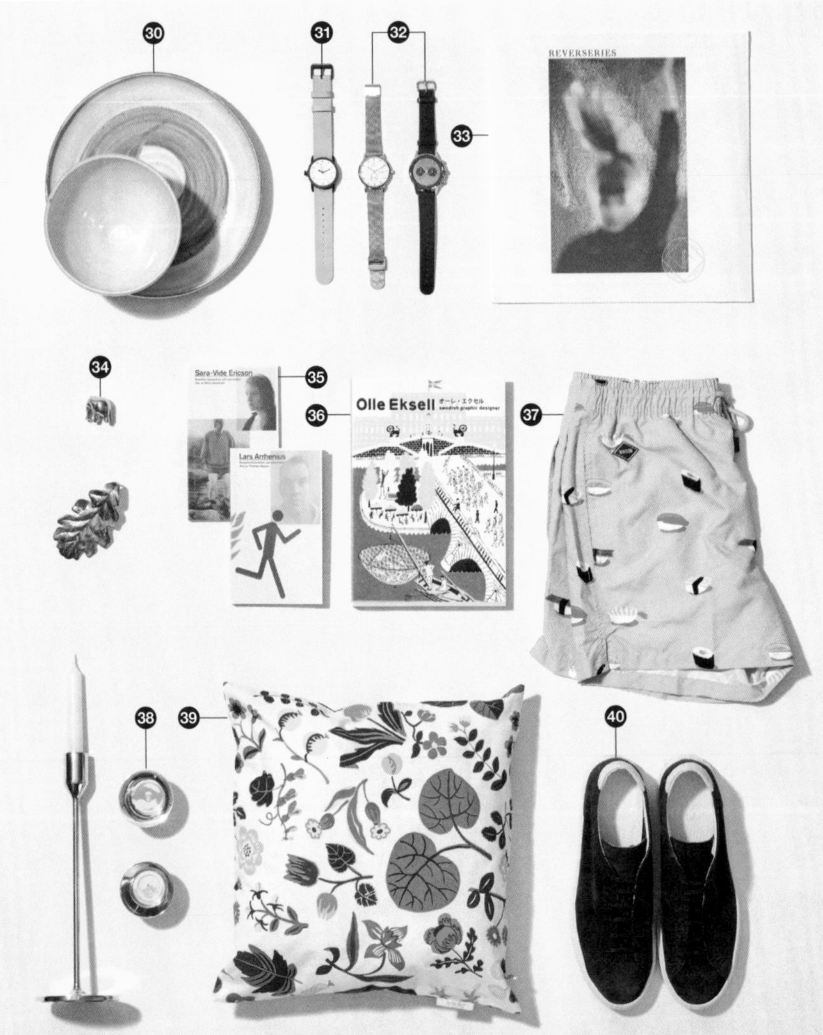

26 Socks by Grandpa
grandpa.se
27 Trainers by Eytys
eytys.com
28 Backpack by Sandqvist
sandqvist.net
29 Low Key clock from Grandpa grandpa.se
30 Austere ceramics from Alma thisisalma.com
31 Watch by Tid
tidwatches.com

32 Watches by Triwa
triwa.com
33 *Reverseries* vinyl by Jennie Abrahamson from Pet Sounds Bar
psb.bar
34 Silver elephant and oak leaf by Svenskt Tenn
svenskttenn.se
35 *Sara-Vide Ericson* by Milou Allerholm and *Lars Arrhenius* by Thomas Olsson (both Orosdi-Back) from Konst-ig konstig.se

36 *Olle Eksell: Swedish Graphic Designer* by Pie Books from Sven-Harrys Konstmuseum
sven-harrys.se
37 Nikben swimming shorts from NK Stockholm nk.se
38 Candle holders by Skultuna
skultuna.com
39 Cushion by Svenskt Tenn
svenskttenn.se
40 Trainers by CQP
c-qp.com

Stockholm
Essays

12 essays
State of Stockholm

Do essays qualify for the literature prize?

1
A short history
View from the plinth
by the late Charles XII of Sweden, monarch

2
Tongue tied
The five stages of learning Swedish
by Stephen Whitlock, writer

3
Life is sweet
Eat like a Swede
by Elna Nykänen Andersson, Monocle

4
Here comes the sun
The changing seasons
by Stella Friberg, writer

5
Heart of darkness
Scandi noir
by Jan Arnald, crime author

6
Winner takes it all
Irresistible pop music
by Fernando Augusto Pacheco, Monocle

7
Shape shifters
Design and architecture
by Andreas Martin-Löf, architect

8
Take a break
The joy of 'fika'
by Anna Brones, writer

9
Quietly confident
Muted fashion stands out
by Jamie Waters, Monocle

10
Social design
Collaborative culture
by Saskia Neuman, curator

11
Pippi power
Literary legacy
Marie-Sophie Schwarzer, Monocle

12
Frank exchange
Josef Frank's legacy
Josh Fehnert, Monocle

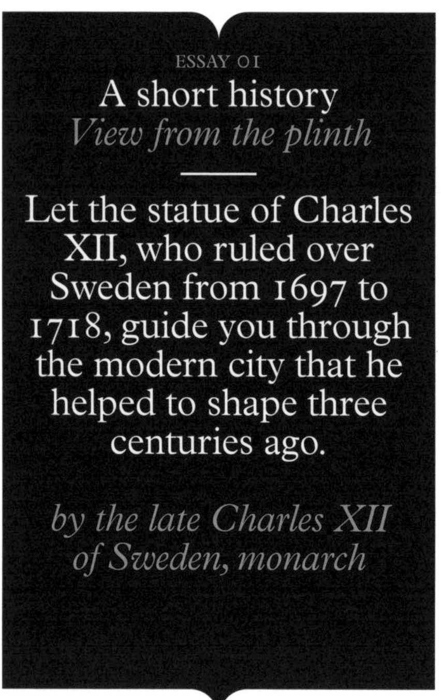

ESSAY 01

A short history
View from the plinth

Let the statue of Charles XII, who ruled over Sweden from 1697 to 1718, guide you through the modern city that he helped to shape three centuries ago.

by the late Charles XII of Sweden, monarch

I know what you're thinking: how do I, Charles XII, stand outside all day in the Swedish winter? The short answer is that we statues do little else. But it's nothing compared to the cold we suffered in Russia. I spent half my life abroad, battling it out in eastern Europe and marching on Moscow. Why do you think I'm pointing east, clutching a sword, surrounded by four mortar cannons? From ascending to the throne as a lad of 15 in 1697 to being killed by a projectile in Norway in 1718, war was my calling.

Now that I've retired to Kungsträdgården I can finally enjoy Stockholm. It took some time getting used to changing fashions and the pigeons doing their business on my epaulettes but I've missed this city. Certainly the winters are long and frosty but it's lovely in springtime, when the cherry trees around the square are in bloom. I'll wager they're no less impressive than the ones in Japan. The city blossoms with them: as soon as the weather looks up, starry-eyed couples walk arm in arm under their pink canopies, kids play football (I should know: I've been hit in the face countless times) and you even get the odd rascal jumping into the harbour. My vantage point is wonderful – who wouldn't want to spend day and night watching over this city?

Let me give you a whistle-stop tour. I can only bear witness to what's happening in front – my stiff back stops me from turning around – but there are worse things than a view of Gamla Stan. There it is, just across the water. It's the birthplace of Sweden as well as my former home. In 1520, in front of what is now the Nobelmuseet on the colourful Stortorget Square, the tyrannical Christian II of Denmark massacred the Swedish nobility in an attempt to subjugate our nation – which was then part of the Kalmar Union, composed of Norway, Sweden and Denmark. But we didn't stand for it. Rebellion had long been coming: a nobleman by the name of Gustav Vasa pushed back the Danish despot in the subsequent War of Liberation and in 1523 established himself as king of an independent Sweden.

But by Thor's hammer! I hope I've not given the wrong impression here. We love our neighbours. Denmark and Norway are our brothers but all siblings have feuds. It's perhaps because we're so close that we waged incessant wars with one another. But we're peaceful nations now. We Swedes have grown up and generally stayed out of trouble since 1814, preferring to look after affairs at home and make amends with the duo next door. I hear that our current king even plays golf every Saturday with Harald V of Norway.

So that's Gamla Stan. I've also been able to turn my attention to the growing skyline of Södermalm, behind the Old Town. Back in the 1700s it was a bohemian and roguish spot: anyone caught here was either a poet or up to no good (or both). Today, I'm told, it's packed with fashionable sorts and well-trimmed beards but the eclectic character is still there. The architecture in particular is a wonderful melting pot, with bright wooden huts cosying up to huge modern behemoths.

"It took some time getting used to changing fashions and the pigeons doing their business on my epaulettes but I've missed this city"

Three more iconic statues in Stockholm

—

01 **Gustav II Adolf**
The King led Sweden to victory during the Thirty Years' War.

02 **Järnpojke**
Touch the head of this tiny iron boy for good luck.

03 **Margaretha Krook**
A heated statue of the beloved Swedish actress.

Where to next? Let's head off to Långholmen. The island to the west of the archipelago has become a popular swimming spot during the summer, with residents keeping boats and cottages along the shore; a better use, I suppose, than the prison it housed until four decades ago. Incarceration is far more in line with the thinking of my later successor Charles XIII (he's situated further up the square). You should hear that traditionalist complaining during the annual 1 May leftwing demonstrations. Yes, you may get an egg in the face and we monarchs certainly wouldn't fare well in these celebrants' system but liberty of thought is the cornerstone of Swedishness: without rebellion, Sweden wouldn't have been born.

That tradition lives on. In 1971 the city proposed chopping down the enormous elm trees around the square to make way for a new metro entrance. A group of youngsters climbed the tree trunks in protest (you can still see the incisions from the chainsaw). And what do you know? The city gave in and moved the entrance. That's the Swedish spirit! Now the main cluster of elms right behind me is home to the *tehuset* (tea house), where a concoction called a "flat white" seems to be the popular choice.

But it's not all politics here. Kungsträdgården is a hoot. When the city isn't frolicking in the sun (we've got to make the most of the summer, a fleeting experience) it's screaming to one modern pop band or another at the concert stage in the middle of the square. The bellowing music isn't to my taste – I far prefer the viola. Further up is a little pool, surrounded by trees, which freezes over in winter and turns into an ice rink. Do grab a pair of skates if you're here around Christmas time. Keep in mind that we Swedes are as comfortable on ice as on the ground so don't be surprised when a little ne'er-do-well zooms past you – backwards.

You ought to see all this for yourself though. Besides, you've been listening to a statue for the past 10 minutes and people are getting suspicious. There are much more interesting things to do in this beautiful city. — (M)

ABOUT THE WRITER: Melkon Charchoglyan is a researcher at MONOCLE. While in Stockholm to report for the travel guide he happily ate four cinnamon buns a day (research) when not interviewing statues.

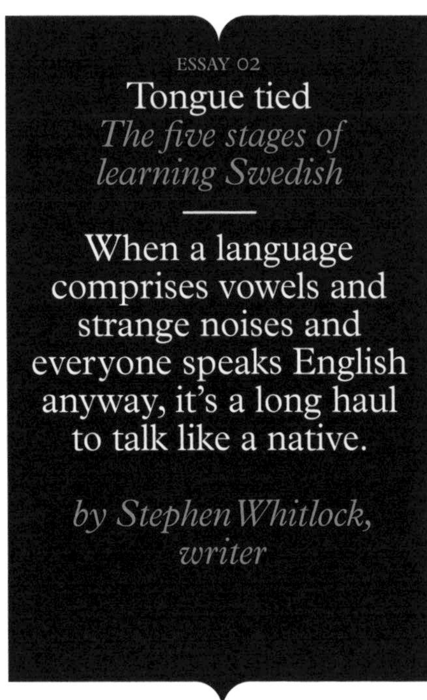

ESSAY 02

Tongue tied

The five stages of learning Swedish

When a language comprises vowels and strange noises and everyone speaks English anyway, it's a long haul to talk like a native.

by Stephen Whitlock, writer

1. Denial

Thank goodness for that: as a new arrival there's no panic language-wise. You don't have to learn Swedish – "I'm sure I'll pick it up along the way but it's not like it's expected of me," you'll reasssure yourself. Stockholmers love speaking English and no one is tetchy when you presume that they can (Paris this isn't). They like to practise and visitors like to be understood so everyone's happy.

And they know their language is a challenge; an exotic soup of vowels and odd sounds that we just don't make in English. You know a language is going to be difficult when the word for seven – *sju* – is a tricky prospect (it's a cross between "shoe", "woo" and the back end of a sneeze). When I'd lived here for a few months not once did anyone ever say that I should be making better progress.

But there was no need: English is everywhere. You can watch Netflix, listen to the BBC World Service and speak English to everyone from the tax office to the fish-seller and they still smile back. You go to dinner parties where you are the only native English speaker at the table yet everyone speaks English all night. You feel bad but they don't mind so it's OK – for now.

2. Anger

I didn't want to be that arrogant English speaker so I signed up at the language school. I was reading children's books by Astrid Lindgren (*see page 89*) and listening to *Chess* and *Mamma Mia!* in Swedish. I made good progress and could say and understand the simple stuff. Yet it took me a year to reach a level that I achieved in three months when I studied Italian. I'd think I was getting somewhere and then in a bar I'd ask for the bill (*notan*) and they'd bring me a bowl of peanuts (*nötter*). I'd politely ask a woman in a restaurant what she was eating ("*Vad äter du?*") and she'd think I was chatting her up by asking for her name ("*Vad heter du?*"). Worse still is when you're stared at blankly. A friend tells me that it is a quirk of Swedish that if you don't get pronunciation just right, Swedes can't hear the word you are saying. Once I asked a taxi driver to take me home to my street. "Arbetargatan," I told him. "Where?" I shifted the emphasis: "*Ar*-betargatan… Ar-*bet*-argatan… Arbe-*tar*-gatan?" On the fifth go I got it right. "Oh, Arbetargatan," he said. "Why didn't you say so?"

> *"I think I'm getting somewhere and then in a bar I ask for the bill (notan) and they bring me a bowl of peanuts (nötter)"*

3. Bargaining

There was progress, even if my reading was better than my conversation and my speaking better than my listening. When I'd chat with friends I used Swedish where I could, while they'd reply in English. The trouble is, it's a bore for them. They'd rather that we all speak English so that the conversation can be fast and funny. I appreciated their patience. Sometimes they'd tell me an anecdote about a friend of a friend who has lived here since the 1960s and still doesn't speak Swedish. It didn't make me feel any better.

4. Depression

After a decade I could chat with friends in Swedish, listen to the radio news in Swedish and write emails in Swedish. Yet on a daily basis I'd go to a café or a shop and give my order in Swedish, perhaps adding a pleasantry about the weather, and they were still answering me in English. They were just trying to be kind but it's a reminder that I'm still an outsider.

5. Acceptance

I'm at peace with the fact that I will never speak Swedish as well as most Swedes speak English. My Scandi pals drop "recalcitrant" and "discombobulated" into conversation without a thought. Even when speaking among themselves they can flip into English to explain something; that's a degree of linguistic amphibiousness that I can only dream of. However, every now and again I do dream in Swedish. And I wake up happy. — (M)

ABOUT THE WRITER: Stephen Whitlock is a Yorkshire-born writer and former TV continuity announcer who moved to Stockholm in 2002. He's written radio drama for the BBC and articles for MONOCLE, *Gardens Illustrated* and *The New York Times*.

ESSAY 03

Life is sweet
Eat like a Swede

Swedish food culture is rooted in its history, traditions and open-minded attitude. And there's one thing that unites everyone: a love of the lingonberry.

by Elna Nykänen Andersson, Monocle

My Swedish husband's Uncle Kurt was born and bred in a small village in northern Sweden called Nordingrå, surrounded by deep forests full of berries. Kurt was a good-natured, generous and entrepreneurial man. In the family he's mainly remembered for two things: the fact that he once owned an ice-cream stand and his unparalleled love of lingonberries. He would eat them with anything and everything. Meatloaf? With berries. Sausage casserole? With berries. Lasagne? You guessed it.

Not all Swedes share Kurt's exceptional appetite for the crimson fruit but most have a dose of lingon love. During my 17 years as a Finn living in Sweden I don't believe I've ever met a Swede who doesn't have a jar of *lingonsylt* (lingonberry jam) somewhere in their fridge. It's also likely that they'll have boxes of the berries in their freezers. Swedes eat them fresh, as a preserve or *rårörda* (tossed with sugar). They'll have them with meatballs, of course, but also with fried herring, potato pancakes, cabbage rolls, waffles, oatmeal, black pudding or as desserts such as chocolate cake or caramel pie.

Let's not forget juice, a drink that Swedes consume by the gallon. And why wouldn't they? In addition to the intense, bittersweet taste, lingonberries are very good for you: a Nordic "superberry", as a recent study by Lund University suggested. Eating them fresh or frozen fuels your system with vitamins A and C, as well as fibre and magnesium.

Food anchors us to our culture. As we grow up we form vivid food memories that become part of our identity. Marcel Proust touched on it in his book *In Search of Lost Time*, with a taste of gâteau madeleine triggering a, well, Proustian rush of childhood memories. For Swedes lingonberries are rooted in culture and history. Swedish food uses lots of ingredients from the forests and the sea, often pickled, smoked or preserved in some way. The practical reason is the long, cold winters when almost nothing can grow. Historically people had to pick as many berries and mushrooms and catch as many fish as they possibly could in order to have food to last until the next summer. That's where Swedish staples such as cured salmon, crispbread and pickled cucumber come in.

"I don't believe I've ever met a Swede who doesn't have a jar of 'lingonsylt' (lingonberry jam) somewhere in their fridge"

Even today, when fresh berries, fruit and mushrooms are readily available in supermarkets year round, foraging in the forests, cooking jam or drying chanterelles are popular pastimes. The classic dishes have survived because they're nostalgic but also because of their great taste. Pickled cucumber, for instance, provides a crispy, fresh contrast to the heavy Swedish *husmanskost* (home-style food) that relies on ingredients such as potatoes, meat and creamy sauces.

"Sweet", by the way, is another key word for Swedes. When I first moved here from my native Finland I noticed how much sweeter almost everything was compared with food back home. The bread was sweet and the Swedes put sugary marmalade on top. Their saccharine yoghurt was eaten with even sweeter granola. At 3 o'clock people often suggested a *fika*: sitting down with friends for cakes and buns washed down with coffee or hot chocolate (*see page 83*).

The average Swedish family, with two adults and two children, eats 1.2kg of sweets per week – most of them on Saturday, which is known as Sweets Day. The reason for this extreme sugar crush can be traced back to the 1930s when the authorities started recommending that people use it in everyday foods. Sugar was produced in Sweden; it was cheap, rich in calories and readily available. In the 1950s the Swedish Medical Board advised that Swedes limit their sweet-intake to once a week but by then it was too late. While most families try to stick to the rule, many are still addicted to the stuff.

Three classic Swedish dishes

01 Gravlax
Cured salmon served with dill, eaten as a starter or snack.

02 Cinnamon buns
An average Swede apparently eats some 300 every year.

03 Gubbröra
Egg-and-anchovy salad often served on rye.

The food culture here also says something about the Swedes' famous openness to other cultures; their curiosity and the multicultural nature of their society. Cabbage rolls, one of the most classic Swedish dishes, were brought to the country by King Charles XII (*see page 70*) from Turkey in the 18th century. Ever since then, Swedes have been enthusiastically incorporating other food cultures into their own, either through their travels or by welcoming immigrants to their country.

France is the country that has had the most profound effect on food here because our nations have historically had close ties. Even the current royal family, the Bernadottes, are of French extraction. After the ubiquitous pizzeria, the most common restaurant in Stockholm is the French-Swedish brasserie, with steak and béarnaise sauce invariably on the menu. But Swedes have also embraced other cultures and ingredients: tacos, pizza and kebabs are all staples of the Swedish diet today. Sometimes the clash of cultures also leads to unique dishes such as the kebab pizza or the taco meat pie; things that might horrify Italians and Mexicans but are much beloved in Sweden. All enjoyed with a healthy dollop of *lingonsylt* of course. — (M)

ABOUT THE WRITER: Elna Nykänen Andersson is MONOCLE's Stockholm correspondent. She also works as a news editor and anchor at Sweden's public broadcaster SVT and is currently writing a cookbook on Swedish food.

ESSAY 04

Here comes the sun
Seasons change

When spring arrives after a long, dark winter, the people of Stockholm embrace the sunlit months with gusto.

by Stella Friberg, writer

We Swedes love talking about the weather. And I don't mean just small talk when stuck in a lift with a stranger: in Sweden the weather is serious business. We are borderline obsessed with the changing of the seasons. It may be a normal minus 5C day in March and pitch black outside but you'll spy us bowling around town in denim jackets and sunglasses. You'll also notice the tone in our voices shifting. Those long, dark winters really do something to us.

The arrival of spring is like the flick of a switch: suddenly you'll see people out on the street again (even on a midweek evening) sitting on benches, stairs and patios all over town with their eyes closed and faces turned towards the sun like sunflowers. It's as if we've all been in hibernation for the winter and can finally thaw and be our best sunniest selves again.

There are a couple of nightclubs in Stockholm – Trädgården and Celezte –

"The long days last all summer and we all thank our lucky stars for that. We need them to fuel up for the winter"

that close for the winter. Their reopening in spring has become the unofficial start of the season and justification for the aforementioned behaviour. Just thinking about these venues makes young Stockholmers' hearts beat a little faster. They represent long nights spent outside listening to music and dancing, topped off, perhaps, with a moonlit swim in Mälaren and walking home barefoot as dawn breaks.

Stockholm in May is hot and full of life. In June you feel the pace slowing down and by midsummer the city has almost reached a standstill. It will remain like this until late August. During this time, many people head out to their cabins in the archipelago – in Torekov, Österlen in Skåne or in Gotland – and settle in for the lazy summer weeks. Most activities are alfresco: barbecues, sunbathing, swimming and biking. Even if the weather leaves a little to be desired (this is still the Baltic after all) you'll see intrepid Swedes wearing lightweight jackets while they freeze in the yard.

For those without a cabin to retreat to, Stockholm is a great summer city. Due to all the waterways and urban islands, most of the things you'd do out of town can be enjoyed in the city: sunbathing and jumping off the cliffs by Fredhällsklipporna; renting canoes and paddleboards for circuits of Kungsholmen Island. Or you can hire a sauna boat (yes, it's as great as it sounds) with friends and chill on the water for a few hours, drink beer in Vitabergsparken or recline in front of the large outdoor cinema screen in Rålambshovsparken.

Midsummer Eve celebrations take place each year on a Friday at the end of June, coinciding with the summer solstice. At the northernmost point of Sweden the sun doesn't set for almost a month before and after midsummer. For us in Stockholm, further down south, it is only around the solstice that we experience the lazy rays of a midnight sun. It starts to set, flirts with the horizon then rises again.

The long days last all summer and we thank our lucky stars for that. We need them to fuel up for the seemingly interminable, dark winter; a time when we drink gallons of coffee and gather at gyms and natural-food joints, attempting to get fit and ready for the summer activities.

You realise that it is totally worth it: you can endure anything in this funny country in the north in order to experience these long summer nights. But come October you'll find us counting down the days again, waiting for Trädgården and Celezte to finally throw open their doors. — (M)

Great places to catch the sun

01 Lydmar Hotel
Soak up the rays on the waterfront patio.
02 Mosebacketerassen
Outdoor bar at Södra Teatern with views over the city.
03 Rosendals Trädgårdkafé
Garden café on Djurgården.

ABOUT THE WRITER: Stella Friberg is a writer and photographer for Scandinavian Airlines (SAS) and its in-flight magazine *Scandinavian Traveler*.

ESSAY 05

Heart of darkness

Scandi noir

The author, otherwise known as Arne Dahl, sets his crime novels in Stockholm. Here he tells us why: to show how his country, beneath the idyllic exterior, is coming to terms with outside forces.

by Jan Arnald, crime author

Sweden has changed. In the 1970s the country tried to isolate itself and at its core was the idea of social democracy: it was the people's home, the welfare state. It never experienced much crime and tried hard to avoid poverty. In short, it was pretty idyllic. But such things depended on it being alone: a peninsula in the north, staying out of wars and keeping well away from global affairs. When globalisation kicked in, the country became more mobile and joined the EU; everything started to shift.

My books in some sense are all about the internationalisation of Sweden. At a certain point it became impossible for us to maintain the old tradition. Lots of Swedish crime fiction from the postwar decades is nostalgic, harking back to a golden age when we, supposedly, took care of everyone and everyone was happy. My books aren't like that: I'm not nostalgic. I believe that the globalisation of Sweden is a good and much needed development. We tended to be a little self-righteous before, the moral conscience of the world, pretending to be that bit better than everyone else.

To me the inspiration behind Swedish crime fiction started with the assassination of prime minister Olof Palme in 1986, a crime that remains unsolved. Back then we believed that it was possible for a prime minister to walk the streets without guards. It was a sign of our naivety. That evening killed not only the prime minister but some measure of Swedish innocence too. It also piqued our interest in solving crimes as everyone became a detective, or harboured a theory.

> *"The fertile ground of Swedish crime fiction came with the assassination of our prime minister, Olof Palme, in 1986"*

Another contributing factor to the emergence of crime fiction is the fact that Sweden has long winters. Most Swedish musicians come from the north because they have little to do during such periods other than sit indoors and strum, blow or pluck. We all look forward to our (albeit) short summers. The hours of darkness and the struggle between light and dark are a natural backdrop for imagined crime.

I chose to pursue crime fiction because I wanted to talk about society. Originally I wrote under my real name and produced works based on the freedom of fantasy. By the time I assumed my pen name, Arne Dahl, I had become more interested in the ways in which society was changing and the liberalism that was taking hold in Sweden. I think the fact that we moved on from the idea of a welfare state changed us more than the influx of people arriving from around the world. The welfare state is still there but it's much changed.

I decided to use Stockholm as the location of this societal shift and my Intercrime series of novels is about the international world coming to our country.

When the Berlin Wall came down all was well but then Russia crept closer and we experienced a new wave of crime as the Russian mafia got a foothold in Stockholm. We then joined the EU, which brought the whole continent closer. At this point Sweden suffered internal turmoil as it came to the realisation that it was not an idyllic world in itself but a country like any other.

Stockholm today is small and easily accessible. It's still somewhat idyllic and the golden-age façade continues to exist in the likes of the Old Town. But behind it lies something more complex: blocks of sombre architecture that echo that of the Soviet Union. The highest castle sits next to the lowest gutter, making it easy to move across the social strata.

I promised myself that I would write 10 books in 10 years and no more – but I've failed miserably. The first 10 were an attempt to follow the development of Stockholm and if you read them you will notice a big difference in the city's outlook. I'm continuing to chart its progress as it moves away from the smaller world of the welfare state to the globalised society that both it and Sweden are today. We've come to embrace it; it feels natural now. And there's no going back. — (M)

More Swedish crime fiction

01 **'Sun Storm' by Åsa Larsson (2003):** Follows a crime-fighting female tax lawyer.
02 **'Firewall' by Henning Mankell (1998):** Detective Kurt Wallander sleuths in Ystad.
03 **'Easy Money' by Jens Lapidus (2012):** Gritty tale of an ill-fated drug deal.

ABOUT THE WRITER: Jan Arnald, known by his penname Arne Dahl, is a Stockholm-born author, journalist and literary critic best known for his Intercrime novel series. His latest English title is *Watching You*.

ESSAY 06

Winner takes it all
Irresistible pop music

From Ace of Base to super-producers and, of course, the mighty Abba, Sweden has given the world more than its fair share of pop mega-hits.

by Fernando Augusto Pacheco, Monocle

It all started the first time I heard "Lucky Love" blasting from the TV in my São Paulo living room, at the tender age of nine. It *was* love: I had fallen head over heels for Ace of Base. It was always destined to be a long-distance relationship but I soon came to realise that a surprising number of my favourite bands hailed from this small, quiet country in the far north, a mere 10,000km away from Brazil. Sweden was a country I knew little about but soon had a great desire to visit. Its melodic ultra-bubblegum Europop was pure perfection to my Brazilian ears.

Although a wave of icy cool Swedish artists such as Tove Lo and Zara Larsson have dominated the airwaves recently, it was the more innocent time when Da Buzz, Carola and Alcazar topped the charts that made my heart go "boom boom" for Sweden.

For such a small country – it has a population of 10 million – the Swedish music market is a resounding international success story. The country is currently the world's third-biggest music exporter and the industry is worth some SEK9.3bn. Stockholm itself has been described as the Silicon Valley of pop music (although a little more fun, I'd imagine). And while Sweden has turned out some great artists there's also a host of fantastic producers, such as Max Martin (the guy behind Britney's "Baby One More Time").

My desire to visit Stockholm became a reality in 2008 but the weather was very, well, "Swedish" and my travelling companions didn't share my enthusiasm for Europop, so it wasn't quite the amorous encounter I had envisaged. However, in one of those incredible twists of fate I ended up (after much petitioning) becoming the Eurovision Song Contest correspondent for Monocle 24 and landed the dream assignment: covering the event in Stockholm.

"The fact that Abba: The Museum is one of the most visited attractions in the city says a lot about how much the Swedes value their musical heritage"

Sure, the Danes and Austrians had done a pretty good job hosting the event in previous years but this was another level: the Swedes treated Eurovision as seriously as a World Cup final. The atmosphere in the spacious Ericsson Globe arena reached fever pitch and the choice of host – a witty entertainer by the name of Petra Mede – was inspired. Plenty of fan areas had been set up around the city too so that all the pop fanatics could get a slice of the action.

Melodifestivalen – the national event held to choose the Swedish contestant – is almost as fiercely competitive as the show itself. Although in other countries Eurovision can be dismissed as a cheesy, camp bit of fun (or an excuse to play drinking games) in Sweden it's a family-friendly event, appreciated by those who enjoy a well-crafted pop song with good lyrics and a catchy hook.

Sweden's relationship with pop music goes beyond Eurovision, of course, but there's no getting away from the fact this is the country that gave the world Abba. To this day I feel proud to share my name with one of their number-one singles: I may be biased but surely "Fernando" is their best hit? And of course, the band has its own venue in Stockholm in the form of Abba: The Museum. It's well deserved after almost 400 million sales across albums and singles.

The fact that it is one of the most visited attractions in the city says a lot about how much the Swedes value their musical heritage.

One of my favourite moments of Eurovision 2016 was a short video medley directed by Jonas Åkerlund. It showcased all the top Swedish hits – including many Abba tracks of course – but also the great Army of Lovers, E-Type and The Cardigans. Even Günther and A*Teens were included. It got me wondering about the Swedes' secret to success: it must be more than just a penchant for a good melody? I would guess that their excellent music education and ease with technology might have more to do with it.

Whatever the reason, they are doing something right. So for now all that's left to say is, Sweden, thank you for the music. — (M)

ABOUT THE WRITER: São Paulo-born Fernando Augusto Pacheco previously worked at Dutch publication *Fantastic Man* and has been enjoying Scandi pop from a young age. He mentions his role as Monocle 24's Eurovision correspondent at every opportunity.

ESSAY 07

Shape shifters

Design and architecture

Known for its pared-back styling and neutral tones, Scandinavian design is undergoing a transformation. Welcome to the second coming of Swedish grace.

by Andreas Martin-Löf, architect

There's a sign at Arlanda Airport that reads: "Welcome to Stockholm, the capital of Scandinavia." It may be a little tongue in cheek but when it comes to design I'd say it's spot on. Copenhagen is perhaps more intimate but Stockholm, home to the largest design week in Scandinavia, is where things actually happen.

The water and the city are one and the same. Stockholm's buildings have a distinctive colour palette. The hues are warm and elegant and the city's architects work hard to maintain their spirit, which entails both preserving and slightly adapting them; after a while it's tedious to put the same colour on a building so we have to refresh them every now and again. And no, we're not fans of white, white, white: it can get *really* cold here in Sweden. We have a long autumn and even longer winter, so we try to create cosy environments where it's pleasant to pass the time. In some countries you socialise in restaurants or public places; in Sweden we invite people into our homes. So here the colour palette is a tool for escaping the length and tedium of winter.

I love the period of Swedish design that developed between 1910 and the breakthrough of modernism in the 1930s, known as Swedish grace or Stockholm classicism. The style is clean with subtle ornamentation and marked the point at which architecture transformed from the heavy, dark brick of national romanticism – Viking-esque and dull – to something altogether more light, airy and classically influenced. Lots of arches, a smattering of friezes and embellishments, plus that less conservative palette. Swedish grace felt somehow more humane and elegant than its forebears.

It was also the very first embodiment of the *folkhemmet* (the welfare state), Sweden's attempt to improve life for all citizens. A lot of housing was built in that style, as well as plenty of public buildings. It is hugely influential on current trends in interior design and architecture, with many designers taking a renewed interest in the reimagining of classical features as part of a modern city.

"It may be controversial but I'd go as far as saying that most contemporary architecture in Sweden is boring"

It may be controversial but I'd go as far as saying that most contemporary architecture in Sweden is boring. There is a young generation of architects in the country trying to analyse the idea of housing and the built environment and improve the situation. Yet over the past few decades we've been building houses that are both low on creativity and technical finesse.

The solution? We shouldn't be afraid of the past. The Swedish and Scandinavian aesthetic as we know it now – muted and pared back – is frightened of its heritage to the point that it's trying to create a *tabula rasa* of expression, free from any influence or tradition. This polemic between the expression of today and of the past is looked on too gravely, with people labelling anything that draws on the past as a pastiche. But a pastiche is something fake and poorly produced. If you execute your task well and add something from your own canon of thought then it's still worthy architecture.

Unique builds

01 Ericsson head office
A glass behemoth split in half by Wingårdhs Arkitektkontor.
02 Aula Medica
The Karolinska Institutet's medical wing.
03 Skogskyrkogården Woodland Crematorium
Gunnar Asplund's 1935 temple-like complex.

I'm excited about the direction that Swedish design is taking. After the financial crisis in 2008 many of the more expensive international brands felt a little lost, which shifted the attention towards newer Danish and Swedish labels. It led to a movement called New Nordic, which was colourful and playful. But it wasn't long before I'd had my fill of that too. The design scene now is moving back towards elegance, human proportions and an equilibrium of colours, as well as the use of longer-lasting materials. In short: a new period of Swedish grace.

Some years ago I travelled to the US with a chair for which I had won an award. An American journalist asked, "What is Scandinavian design?" I stupidly answered that there was no longer such a thing, that we were on the first step to a global, homogenous design. But I'll admit that I've been proven wrong. Travel around the world and you'll realise that the inherent differences of expression – design included – are as apparent as ever. At the same time, with the globalisation of the world through international trade fairs (such as the one in Stockholm each February) and the arrival of the internet, people can now connect with one another and appreciate different movements in new ways. So yes, in that sense design has become more globalised because someone in Sweden can understand and appreciate something from Brazil or India; design is both tribal and part of a broader whole.

I'm non-partisan on the issue. If you ask me whether to buy Danish or Swedish my answer is: buy something beautiful. There's no reason why I should convince you to buy one over the other just for the sake of it. And I certainly don't think that the world's interest in Scandinavian design is a fleeting moment. It develops and changes; after all, this is a region that has been at the top of its game for a long time – and will be for decades to come. — (M)

ABOUT THE WRITER: Andreas Martin-Löf is a Stockholm-based architect and designer. In 2008 he founded Andreas Martin-Löf Arkitekter, which today is one of our favourite young architectural practices in Sweden.

ESSAY 08

Take a break
The joy of 'fika'

A good cup of coffee, a freshly baked pastry or cake and time out with good company: here's an everyday tradition that's worth embracing.

by Anna Brones, writer

Whether it's a grey and gloomy winter day (hands jammed into jacket pockets and scarf pulled up to the eyes) or one of those precious first weeks of the summer season (sunglasses on and scarf off), in Stockholm there's only one drink of choice: coffee.

A visitor need only spend a few hours in Stockholm before they are introduced to *fika*, one of the most common and yet special Swedish traditions. Both a noun and a verb, *fika* is fundamentally a coffee break: a moment of respite when one's full attention is given to the coffee cup, a sweet treat and a friend's company.

Sweden has a close bond with coffee. In fact, it's Scandinavians who drink the most of the black stuff (along with the Dutch) in northern Europe. Coffee is an excuse for a break or a social call. A visit to a Swede's house will inevitably involve the offering of it and something tasty to go alongside. Meanwhile, a journey to the *konditori* (pastry shop) for caffeine served in a porcelain cup alongside a delicate pastry isn't merely a stop on a long list of errands but an outing in its own right.

Sweden isn't unique in celebrating the coffee break but it is unique in how it does so. *Fika* is a chance to check out from the daily routine if only for a few moments. It can be done anywhere, at any time and with anyone. It is the activity that spans all ages and all manner of folk.

It's impossible to understand Stockholm without *fika*; the social ritual is part of the driving force behind the city's booming café culture. Pop into any of Stockholm's cafés in the winter and you'll see people nursing a large mug of coffee, a quiet warmth emanating from the space while the cold weather envelops the streets outside. In late winter, bakeries duel it out with their *semlor*: the cardamom buns filled with cream and almond paste that make for an indulgent *fika* before Lent. On a summer afternoon, stroll through the heart of Södermalm and observe the crowds spilling out onto the terraces, mugs in hand, in order to soak up the long-awaited sunshine.

While in some countries we might ask a friend if they want to grab a coffee, asking a Swede "*Ska vi fika*?" is loaded with much more social meaning. *Fika* is never coffee in a takeaway cup, consumed quickly at a desk. It's not the caffeine fix that a coffee addict needs in the morning. Instead *fika* provides an opportunity to slow down. It is a social activity, the chance to talk about something other than work with colleagues or the time to catch up with a friend. It can be a solo pursuit too; a quiet moment for you, your cup and your thoughts. In a sense *fika* is a celebration of the everyday, a contemplative moment to be savoured.

> *"Fika is a celebration of the everyday, a joyful moment to be savoured"*

In a country known for its modesty and restraint, it's a salubrious exception. It is such a common part of the Swedish routine – workers are used to a break in the morning *and* the early afternoon, commonly spent with co-workers, perhaps with a treat from the bakery or, better yet, baked at home – that many Swedes wouldn't think of the custom as extraordinary. But you have only to look at the recent popularity of *fika*-themed cafés around the world to realise that once Swedes leave their homeland they often miss the magic of this idiosyncratic coffee break – and that foreigners are keen to mimic its charms.

Stockholm is the home of *fika*. The city is peppered with bakeries and cafés, both new and old. Classics such as Vete-Katten (*see page 38*) have been serving traditional *fika* since the 1920s and newer speciality cafés such as Drop Coffee (*see page 39*) are challenging coffee norms, offering an alternative to the strong, dark brew that Swedes adore.

It's not a difficult concept to embrace. After all, no matter where you take it, *fika* offers the ultimate lesson to travellers: sit down and enjoy the moment. — (M)

Swedish coffee terms

—

01 **'Fikastund'**
A *fika* moment.
02 **'Kaffebröd'**
Literally "coffee bread", referring to any pastry served with coffee.
03 **'Påtår'**
A coffee refill.

ABOUT THE WRITER: Anna Brones is a freelance writer and founder of the blog *Foodie Underground*. She has recently written a book on how Swedes take their brew: *Fika: The Art of the Swedish Coffee Break*.

ESSAY 09

Quietly confident

Muted fashion stands out

—

In a world where fashion houses scream for attention with evermore ostentatious creations, Stockholm's sartorial restraint is a soothing sight for sore eyes.

by Jamie Waters, Monocle

When pounding the pavements of Stockholm you will notice scores of men and women dressed oh-so-elegantly in jackets and trousers in muted combinations of grey, beige and black. You will see rails of these pared-back clothes when you enter the flagships of the city's marquee labels, be it Filippa K, J Lindeberg or Our Legacy. This sleek simplicity is particular to Swedish, rather than Scandinavian, fashion (the Danes are far more streetwear-y and up for a sloganed sweater). It is even more particular to the fashion of Stockholm, a city in which understated dressing is an unwritten rule and where not standing out is a decades-long tradition.

Such dressing is aligned with the Law of Jante: the Nordic social concept that advocates never being flashy or sticking out. This Scandi version of "tall-poppy syndrome" has historic roots across the region but became deeply ingrained in Sweden (where it is called *jantelagen*) during the 44-year-long domination of the Social Democratic party (from 1932 to 1976). Under the reigns of prime ministers Tage Erlander and Olof Palme, capitalism was condemned and the collective prioritised above the individual. By the time Palme was assassinated, this line of thinking had shaped the nation's psyche – including the way people dress.

"With few flourishes at their disposal, the city's designers have had to dazzle consumers by nailing the basics: details, fabrics and cuts are everything"

"The *jante* mindset has had an influence on Swedish fashion for sure," says Alexander Stutterheim, one of today's masters of stripped-back clothing. His eponymous raincoat label has captured the affections of dapper consumers with its restrained designs in charcoal and ecru tones, and in 2016 he launched John Sterner, a knitwear brand comprising similarly quiet pieces. "When a design is more neutral it doesn't draw too much attention from the person wearing it," he says. "We love simplicity in Sweden and the colour black, which is *jante* put into a fashion context."

Countless other homegrown labels – from high street to high fashion – have turned this minimalist look into winning formulas. (There are other factors at play here too: for instance, many designers say that Sweden's cold, grey weather encourages them to favour practicality and muted tones over bright colours.) H&M, the fast-fashion giant, perhaps encapsulates *jante* better than any other label: its pieces are basic, affordable and the antithesis of exclusivity. In the design world, Ikea is on a par.

More high-end designers who have built their fortunes on minimalism include Ann-Sofie Back, who has explicitly referenced *jante* as an influence behind collections of monochromatic draped dresses and trouser suits. Then there's Uniforms for the Dedicated – with its logo-less, block-colour men's sweaters – and Acne Studios, especially in the late 1990s when it started out with a pair of indigo jeans. Meanwhile, in a small space in Östermalm, young tailoring firm Saman Amel is applying this thinking to suits. "It's not like you walk into the party and you're a showstopper. But if somebody takes the time to look at you, they'll see that what you're wearing just works," says co-founder Dag Granath of its bespoke designs, which come in tasteful greys, beiges and blues – and, notably, not in patterns.

The term *jantelagen* often has negative connotations and younger generations of Swedes consider it a dated word. However, the principle underpinning it – not being ostentatious – is as relevant as ever. "Today Swedish people are afraid to make a statement about what they are wearing and, especially in central parts of Stockholm, everybody looks the same," says Granath. "If you go to a party around Östermalm, everyone will be wearing trainers, Acne jeans, a white T-shirt, an exclusive watch, maybe a jacket – but all pretty toned down."

This is hardly a bad thing – quite the opposite, in fact. With few flourishes at their disposal, the city's designers have had to dazzle consumers by nailing the basics: details, fabrics and cuts are

Stockholm's top multibrand shops

01 Nitty Gritty
The best spread of men's and women's streetwear brands.

02 Keen
Elegant designs for women.

03 Skoaktiebolaget
Well-heeled men flock to this shoe shop for UK and Italian footwear.

everything. The popularity of Stutterheim's macs depends on simple matte finishes, snap-back buttons and white cotton drawstrings. And Saman Amel's suits will sell only if their fit – slim yet slightly heavier than the Neapolitan style – is spot on. "Some people might consider it boring but personally I think it's drawing attention to what is most crucial," says Granath.

Each season fashion houses in London, New York and Paris release ever more eccentric designs that are embraced by bloggers, Instagrammers et al. Grabbing attention – eliciting "likes", "shares" and "retweets" – is the name of the fashion game. Against this backdrop of sartorial screaming, Stockholm's simple, chic dressing is a refreshing tonic. And, rather ironically, its designers stand out on the international stage all the more because their creations are so restrained and quietly self-confident. Sometimes a thoughtful whisper is far louder than a meaningless shout. — (M)

ABOUT THE WRITER: Jamie Waters writes about fashion for MONOCLE and leapt at the chance to visit Stockholm, home to his favourite labels Acne and Our Legacy. He edited the Retail chapter, which meant plenty of conversations with dapper shop owners.

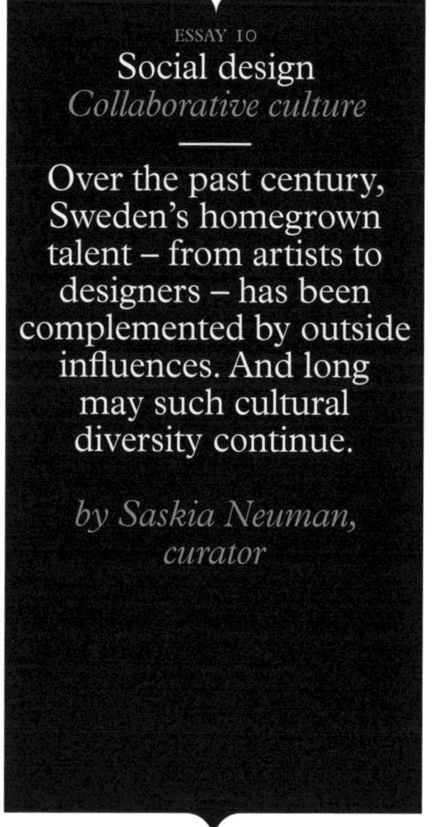

ESSAY 10

Social design

Collaborative culture

Over the past century, Sweden's homegrown talent – from artists to designers – has been complemented by outside influences. And long may such cultural diversity continue.

by Saskia Neuman, curator

Examples of the Swedish design aesthetic disseminating around the globe throughout the 20th century are plentiful. For a country of its size, Sweden has produced a surprising number of fashion labels: you need only look at the average high street to recognise its exports, from H&M to Acne.

Then, of course, there's Ikea: founded in 1943, the company has long been the world's biggest manufacturer of flat-packed furniture (as well as the producer of one of its most widely circulated publications: the Ikea catalogue). It's the perfect example of how Swedish creativity has been paired with the country's utilitarian ideals to produce functional, elegant and affordable design for all. But while Sweden has a rich design heritage propagated by some incredible homegrown talent, a brief look at the past century reveals that outside influences have been equally important.

After the Second World War, while Europe was rebuilding, Sweden was able to quickly shift focus from wartime refuge to progressive poster child of the modern state. It relished postwar economic expansion and, as US goods flooded the Swedish market in the 1950s, Swedes had the cash with which to purchase. A hunger for popular culture developed and Sweden started looking to the US, and later the UK, for fashion, music and art.

This is evident in the Moderna Museet (*see page 94*). In the 1960s its director Pontus Hultén introduced pop art to Sweden. He was the first curator to exhibit a large collection of Andy Warhol's work in Europe and also curated exhibitions exposing great US artists such as Jasper Johns and Robert Rauschenberg to the Swedish public.

In recent years, private art museums have sprouted to accompany several state-funded institutions, making artistic discourse from abroad even more available and diverse. The socially conscious political narrative has meant healthy funding for the arts too.

An interest in international culture keeps Sweden versatile. Having previously been a country of emigrants, in the 1970s Sweden had to import workers from southern European countries, including Greece, Italy and former Yugoslavia. And with new people came new cultures.

"After the Second World War, Sweden was able to quickly shift focus from wartime refuge to progressive poster child of the modern state"

This wasn't an entirely new phenomenon. Svenskt Tenn, whose fabric patterns are often heralded as being the epitome of Swedish design, in fact had Austrian immigrant Josef Frank (*see page 91*) as head designer throughout the second half of the 20th century.

But today the Swedish intellectual aesthetic is under threat. Sweden is marked by the same right-wing jolt that's prevalent in other historically liberal European countries.

Devoid of resistance, hardship and tribulation, Stockholm's cultural offerings were able to thrive, welcoming foreign influence and gaining gravitas

Flat-pack king

01 **Going global**
Ikea operates 340 shops in 28 countries.

02 **Piling on the products**
There are 12,000 of them across the Ikea range.

03 **Working it**
Ikea has 163,000 employees worldwide.

abroad. However, faced with more foreign influences and more people, this has slowly faltered. The nationalistic Sweden Democrats party is keen to preserve "Swedish culture" but its anti-liberal stance puts all cultural outlets at risk. Whether it is the freedom to exhibit whatever art the museum chooses or a community centre's choice to explore whatever foreign culture it represents, expressions of Swedish culture are many and varied.

Sweden has a difficult journey ahead. My hope is that it continues to champion cultural diversity as it always has, rather than try to preserve something insular that it has outgrown. — (M)

i

ABOUT THE WRITER: Saskia Neuman is a curator and director of the Absolut Art Award. She has previously worked at the KW Institute for Contemporary Art in Berlin and the 2009 Venice Biennale.

ESSAY 11

Pippi power

Literary legacy

Long before the country's crime writers became the darlings of the literary scene, Sweden's most famous little girl was charming readers across the world.

by Marie-Sophie Schwarzer, Monocle

Before Nordic noir won over readers across the globe, it was a little girl with red pigtails and a monkey called Mr Nilsson doing much of the literary heavy lifting. Her name is Pippi Longstocking and she's the creation of Astrid Lindgren who, until her death in 2002, spent most of her life in Stockholm. The character she brought to life has become a Swedish icon and indelibly linked to the country's quirky culture.

Lindgren's fictional world is one of endless possibilities: an idealised version of the author's childhood that makes for an enduring endorsement of the nation. With more than 160 million books sold to date, Lindgren's stories not only contribute to Sweden's ample soft-power reserves but also helped put the Nordic nation on the literary map long before the crime screeds.

Though Pippi was published in 1945, the series foreshadows Sweden's standing as one of the world's most progressive countries; not for nothing is the northern nation regularly ranked highly for gender

Read all about it

01 Crime fiction
The Hypnotist by Alexander and Alexandra Coelho Ahndoril (who write as Lars Kepler).
02 Historical fiction
Simon and the Oaks by Marianne Fredriksson.
03 Nobel prize winner
The Dwarf by Pär Lagerkvist.

equality. Pippi's world is the picture of emancipation. When her friend Tommy asks her why she's walking backwards, she says, "Isn't this a free country? Can't a person walk any way she wants to?"

For brand Sweden, Pippi is a charming mascot and her popularity unparalleled. No Swedish author has been translated into as many languages as Lindgren and, considering that Swedish is one of the world's 10 most-translated languages in fiction, it's no small feat.

In fact, despite global uncertainty in the industry, Sweden's sway in the international publishing market is on the up, with record numbers of applications for translation grants rolling in and export sales of Swedish novels bringing in more than €3m a year. Though Pippi can only take so much credit, one reason for Sweden's literary might is the booming crime genre, spurred on by Stieg Larsson's Millennium trilogy. Following Maj Sjöwall and Per Wahlöö (pioneers of Swedish crime fiction), Larsson divulged the shadier side of Swedish life.

"Pippi may have started out as a simple bedtime story but today she's a hero"

Lindgren herself admitted that her own life wasn't the idyll she portrayed through Pippi. "You can be as sad as can be but, when you write, everything vanishes," she said. With Stockholm's average of 164 days of rain, it's not hard to imagine the delight she took in conjuring summer, while Larsson likely found inspiration in Sweden's darker days.

His female protagonist, Lisbeth Salander, is a literary anti-hero to fearless Pippi – today it's the more realistic lead that shifts novels. This too is the case with Henning Mankell's deeply flawed inspector Kurt Wallander, whose tales have sold 30 million copies.

Nordic noir has emerged from the shadows as a multimillion-dollar industry and it even has its own organisation to promote the genre: the Swedish Crime Writers' Academy. Of course, the most prestigious of prizes in Sweden is the Nobel prize for literature (which, pub quizzers, has gone to eight Swedish writers since the prize began in 1901).

Though Lindgren never scooped a Nobel prize, she did win the Peace prize of the German Book Trade in 1978 thanks to her novels and political activism. In her widely broadcast acceptance speech she spoke out against violence towards children, which ultimately led Sweden to ban corporate punishment as the world's first country the following year.

Whether or not you've encountered Pippi, she continues to be a source of quiet inspiration to many and a reflection of the pioneering writer and activist who created her. Pippi may have started out as a simple bedtime story but today she's a hero for readers and for Sweden too. And while Larsson's anti-hero is far removed from the little girl with the knee-high socks, it holds true that whatever the genre, Swedish literature continues to draw people into the nation that inspired it. It certainly got me hooked. — (M)

ABOUT THE WRITER: Marie-Sophie Schwarzer is an associate editor at MONOCLE. She grew up on Pippi Longstocking (it was her go-to carnival costume for years) and she was delighted to visit the city where Astrid Lindgren came up with the colourful character.

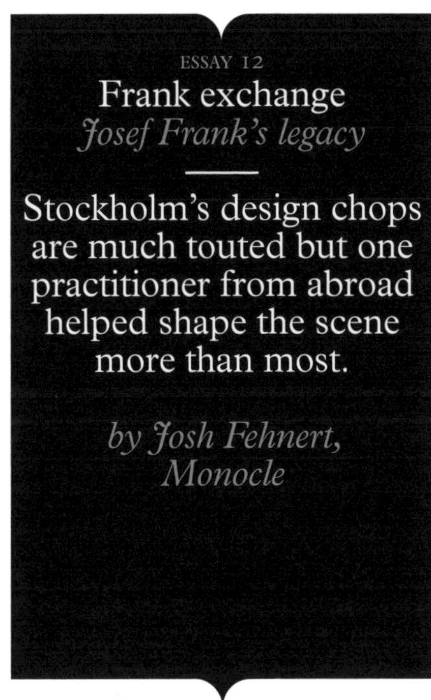

ESSAY 12

Frank exchange

Josef Frank's legacy

Stockholm's design chops are much touted but one practitioner from abroad helped shape the scene more than most.

by Josh Fehnert, Monocle

Forget flat-packed furniture and modish minimalism: Swedish design is a more interesting, expressive beast than those clichés suggest. To prove this point you need only venture as far as an unassuming waterside shopfront on Strandvägen, Östermalm. Here you'll see a squiggle of white cursive script on a blue sign reading "Svenskt Tenn" ("Swedish Pewter"). But inside there's an altogether more nuanced portrait of Swedish design.

The shop is a rolling, labyrinthine affair brimming with colourful, clashing and cacophonous patterns. There are spindly legged chairs, teetering lamps and plush sofas the size of hatchbacks, as well as textiles adorned with beaky birds, plump fruit and forests of foliage. It's a visual symphony and a fairly noisy affront to the austere lines and quiet minimalism for which Scandi style is now known. What's more, the man behind much of the decorative melee channelled the adulation of a nation that accommodated him when he was left stateless.

Josef Frank was born in Austria in 1885 and educated in Vienna at a time of extreme upheaval and foment (Freud, Loos, Klimt and others were among the pillars of culture who dwelt here). The scion of a Jewish family, Frank showed promise as an architect before interning in Berlin in 1908. Here he encountered a young Charles-Édouard Jeanneret (later known as Le Corbusier), as well as architects Mies van der Rohe, Walter Gropius and Peter Behrens.

> *"It's a fairly noisy affront to the austere lines and quiet minimalism for which Scandi style is now known"*

It was in Berlin that Frank first fell for Sweden, this time in the form of a music student called Anna Sebenius (five years his senior) who would become his wife and near life-long companion. All seemed set for him until, in an event that would foreshadow his eventual relocation to Sweden, the

First World War upended the young designer's world.

After the war, as the economic uncertainty of the Wall Street Crash bit deeper in the early 1930s and Hitler swept to power in Germany, Frank fled. When Germany finally claimed Austria in the Anschluss of 1938, he succeeded in gaining Swedish citizenship the following year. This act of kindness ultimately influenced the trajectory of Frank's work and his immigrant's love of his adopted homeland.

He moved to an apartment on Rindögatan, near Svenskt Tenn, and began what would become an almost three-decade collaboration with its owner, Estrid Ericson. Whereas in Vienna the boundaries of modernism had been drawn, in Sweden Frank was able to follow his own rules. He cast off the cudgels of mass production in favour of craft, espoused the beauty of nature over industry and sentimentalism over rationality. Stockholm was the backdrop but it was also the genesis. His work encompassed cushions, throws, armoires and objets d'art that were festooned with bright fabrics and peppered with primary colours. Many of these continue to adorn the still-open shop, as well as better appointed Swedish homes across the nation.

Frank himself didn't realise the importance of his work. In his view furnishings needed to be replaced regularly and he conceded that his own pieces may only be around for a generation. This observation has been proved wrong by their continued popularity.

Whatever his origin, Frank's work remains indelibly Swedish – and the Swedes agree. His patterns and pieces of furniture grace Swedish foreign ministries and royal residences and even featured in a blockbuster Nationalmuseum show during his own lifetime (unheard of for a living artist, let alone a foreigner).

It's curious that newcomers to a city can sometimes see its promise more clearly than its residents. It's stranger still that an Austrian émigré could create a body of work that has so influenced and distilled what it means to be Swedish today. More so than a Billy bookcase or flat-packed wardrobe from Ikea ever could. — (M)

Reading on Frank

01 **'Josef Frank: The Unknown Watercolours'**
Published by Nicotext.
02 **'Josef Frank'**
By Hedvig Hedqvist; published by Orosdi-Back.
03 **'Accidentism: Josef Frank'**
By Mikael Bergquist and Olof Michelsen; published by Birkhäuser.

ABOUT THE WRITER: Josh Fehnert is MONOCLE's food and travel editor and visited Stockholm (he insisted on several trips) to report and oversee this guide. His favourite Frank design? The verdant fruit-like Celotocaulis pattern, ideally on a cosy cushion.

Culture
Art of the city

Countries with regal roots such as Sweden can wear their cultural offerings a little heavily for our tastes; sometimes they can come across as a mite stuffy or precious about their cultural clout. But not Stockholm.

While the old gems shine as brightly as ever there's also an exciting clutch of private galleries in Vasastan, as well as the world-class Moderna Museet on an island (Skeppsholmen), where it's easy to spend a day with the masters of art, sculpture and design. Then there are flashes of inspiration such as the Fotografiska, a peerless paean to both photography and reinvention (before it opened in 2010, the area it occupies wasn't much to behold).

Here's our portrait of a cultural spread that's mastered the art of the museum, jazz bar, nightclub and many other venues in between.

Museums
Must-see collections

1

Artipelag, Gustavsberg
Into the woods

A 20-minute drive from the city proper you'll find architect Johan Nyrén's Artipelag art gallery, tucked away in a glade surrounded by forest. There are four main spaces that host exhibitions, past examples of which have included furniture designed by Mats Theselius, fashion by Lars Wallin and an Andy Warhol retrospective.

The shop stocks Artipelag's own creations including ceramics and tote bags. Summer sees the opening of the 1,100-seat Artbox music hall for everything from grungey gigs to opera.

1 Artipelagstigen, 134 40
+46 (0)8 5701 3000
artipelag.se

Great galleries

The stretch of Hornsgatan nearest to central Södermalm is the unofficial gallery quarter. Big players in Vasastan may attract the prestige but the galleries here offer a variety of lesser-known works. Many painters have their studios here too, so you might catch a master at work.

Three must-see museums

01 **Nobelmuseet, Gamla Stan:** Upon his death in 1896, chemist and businessman Alfred Nobel (who also invented dynamite) asked that some of his fortune be distributed every year to pioneers in fields from chemistry to literature. The museum, opened in 2001, charts the worthy work of the winners.
nobelmuseum.se

02 **Vasamuseet, Djurgården:** This purpose-built structure houses the well-preserved Vasa warship. A monstrous galleon commissioned by King Gustavus Adolphus, it sunk in Stockholm harbour on its maiden voyage in 1628. It was salvaged 333 years later.
vasamuseet.se

03 **Nordiska Museet, Djurgården:** The first thing you see inside this neo-renaissance pile is a statue of King Gustav Vasa but the exhibits aren't just stuffy history lessons. There are exhibitions on topics such as the Aurora Borealis (northern lights) and Nordic design too.
nordiskamuseet.se

Moderna Museet, Skeppsholmen
Modern master

With the pick of the city's art (Picasso, Dalí, Duchamp, Matisse and Rauschenberg among them), Moderna Museet opened in 1958 and moved to its current digs (courtesy of Spanish architect Rafael Moneo) in 1998. The Pontus Hultén Study Gallery was designed by Renzo Piano and named after the late director, who bequeathed hundreds of works.

There are also sculptures by the likes of Alexander Calder and Bjørn Nørgaard. The museum's permanent collection is free but special exhibitions cost extra.
4 Exercisplan, 111 49
+46 (0)8 5202 3500
modernamuseet.se

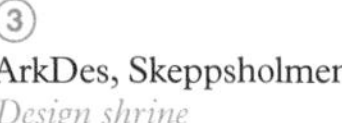

③
ArkDes, Skeppsholmen
Design shrine

Sweden's largest architecture museum explores the link between design and society through exhibitions, seminars and debates (and, in practice, through the extension by architect Rafael Moneo). Its permanent exhibition examines the Swedish vernacular through the ages, while special shows cover both young upstarts and old masters.

The archive of models, photos and drawings from some 500 architects is a treasure trove for design aficionados, while on-site Café Blom is great for refreshments.
4 Exercisplan, 111 49
+46 (0)8 5202 3500
arkdes.se

4

Royal Palace, Gamla Stan
Italian baroque

Still home to Swedish royals, much of this 18th-century baroque building is open to the public. The façade is the handiwork of architect Nicodemus Tessin the Younger and inside are 600 rooms, including a museum of antiquities compiled by Gustav III, housing more than 200 Greek and Roman sculptures acquired during a grand tour of Italy in the late 18th century.

The best views of this hulking beast are from across the water on Södra Blasieholmshamnen in Östermalm, particularly when the sun dips and the spotlights spark up.
1 Slottsbacken, 111 30
+46 (0)8 402 6130
kungahuset.se

5

Sven-Harrys Konstmuseum, Vasastan
Do it yourself

Sven-Harry Karlsson didn't want to donate his art to a museum that he feared might stuff it in a dusty basement. His alternative? To build his own. Opened in 2011, this brassy six-floor behemoth has a mirrored walkway that greets and confuses visitors in equal measure, and which is only surpassed in strangeness by Karlsson's recessed top-floor apartment. Created by Anna Höglund, the building is in perpetual danger of overshadowing the changing exhibitions within.
10-12 Eastmansvägen, 116 61
+46 (0)8 5116 0060
sven-harrys.se

Three more royal palaces

01 **Drottningholm Palace, Drottningholm:** This Unesco World Heritage site, built in the 1680s by Queen Hedwig Eleonora, is the best kept of the royal dwellings. The theatre holds public opera shows.
kungahuset.se

02 **Ulriksdal Palace, Ulriksdal:** This modest 17th-century palace was owned by a general and courtier of Queen Kristina. Don't miss the sculpture collection in the Orangery.
kungahuset.se

03 **Rosendal Palace, Djurgården:** This pink castle (which only opens in summer) has changed little since the 1820s. Its colourful salons are a window into the era.
kungahuset.se

⑥
Thielska Galleriet, Djurgården
Patron of the arts

Behind many a decent artist lurks a patient patron – in this case the late banker Ernest Thiel. When times were good he enlisted architect Ferdinand Boberg to build an art nouveau residence in the sleepy eastern reaches of Djurgården but when his fortunes turned his house, and the art within, were ceded to the government and opened to the public in 1926.

Inside is a glut of turn-of-the-century Nordic art, including works by Edvard Munch. Before leaving, head into the garden to glimpse sculptures by Auguste Rodin.
8 Sjötullsbacken, 115 25
+46 (0)8 662 5884
thielskagalleriet.se

Public galleries
Many and varied

Fotografiska, Södermalm
Point and click

The Fotografiska sits in a picturesque spot a few minutes walk from Slussen Station. Opened in 2010 by brothers Per and Jan Broman, the former customs house has four large galleries and about 20 smaller spaces devoted to a changing roster of the world's best shutterbugs.

The city stumped up SEK250m for the art nouveau-style building's restoration and its character hits an appealing middle ground between flashy and understated. The café-bar and restaurant offer panoramic views over the water.
22 Stadsgårdshamnen, 116 45
+46 (0)8 5090 0500
fotografiska.eu

②
Kulturhuset, Norrmalm
Culture club

Architect Peter Celsing built the sprawling modernist-style Kulturhuset (Culture House) in the 1970s and, as the broad name suggests, its functions are manifold. It's been home to Stockholm City Theatre since 1990 and was used as a makeshift parliament building while the Riksdag was remodelled in the early 1980s.

Nowadays the building accommodates a dance troupe, film screens and libraries. It also hosts seminars and exhibitions, which have included the works of Patti Smith and Robin Rhode.

Sergels torg, 111 57
+46 (0)8 5062 0212
kulturhusetstadsteatern.se

③
Magasin III, Frihamnen
Installation specialists

This exhibition space, directed by David Neuman, has amassed a fine collection of works, including James Turrell's "Dawning" (an optical illusion resembling a painted canvas) and video-art installations by Tony Oursler.

The gallery is also preparing for a slap-up relaunch. "We want to pause to rethink the institution and how we can show art in an even more contemporary and exciting way," says curator Tessa Praun. From September 2017, access is by appointment while a conceptual rethink is underway.

28 Frihamnsgatan, 115 56
+46 (0)8 5456 8040
magasin3.com

Bonniers Konsthall, Vasastan
Accessible art

Contemporary art can feel inaccessible and cryptic (sharks in formaldehyde are fishy business after all) but Bonniers Konsthall is bent on dispelling the illusion with free and varied exhibitions. The five-storey Johan Celsing-designed building has hosted an exhibition on insomnia, welcomed installations by Susan Philipsz and considered the changing role of cities through a photography display called *City Walks*. Those yearning for a deeper insight can drop in for a free guided tour by the learned team.
19 Torsgatan, 113 21
+46 (0)8 736 4248
bonnierskonsthall.se

Liljevalchs Konsthall, Djurgården
Groundbreaking gallery

Liljevalchs was the first independent gallery for contemporary art in Sweden. Housed in a building by architect Carl Bergsten, the gallery showcases about four art exhibitions per year by artists and designers, from sculptor Berit Lindfeldt to fashion designer Ann-Sofie Back. Its Spring Salon is a particular highlight.

At the time of this guide going to print the main building is closed for renovation. It's set to reopen in January 2018 and the Gert Wingårdh extension will follow in 2020.
60 Djurgårdsvägen, 115 21
+46 (0)8 5083 1330
liljevalchs.se

⑥

Färgfabriken, Liljeholmen
Young talent

Perched beyond the western tip of Södermalm, this vast former paint factory has coloured the city's contemporary-art scene since opening in 1995. Exhibits regularly lunge between styles and disciplines and the place has an admirable pedigree for risking its reputation on young Nordic talent.

Past shows have included Canadian-born Carl Johan De Geer and the rabble-rousing Maurizio Cattelan, whose satirical installations include a piece depicting Pope John Paul II having been pummelled by a meteorite.
1 Lövholmsbrinken, 117 43
+46 (0)8 645 0707
fargfabriken.se

Mindepartementet Art and Photography, Skeppsholmen
Intimate portrait

Despite being flanked by the Moderna Museet and ArkDes (*see page 94*), Mindepartementet holds its own. From the 1730s it served as a storehouse for the navy but fell into disuse in the 1980s.

The photo gallery took residence in 2016 and houses a permanent collection dedicated to Christer Strömholm's black-and-white portraits from the 1960s. It also hosts talks and exhibitions in other mediums. Sink your teeth into national delicacies at the top-notch café.
26 Slupskjulsvägen, 111 49
+46 (0)8 611 6969
mindepartementet.org

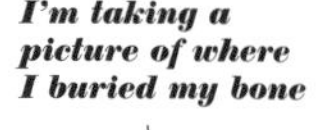

Commercial galleries
Championing emerging artists

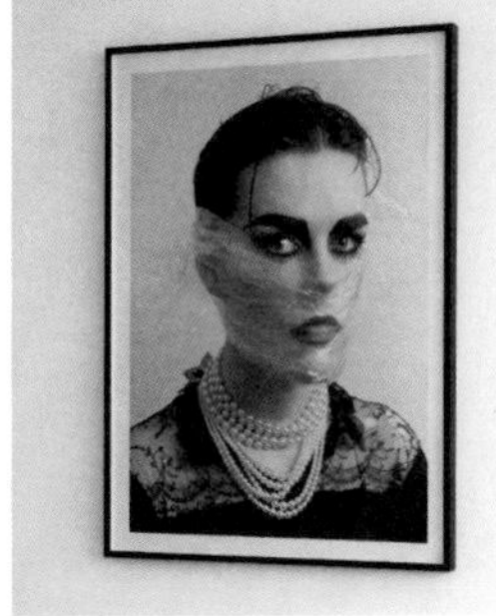

① Andréhn-Schiptjenko, Vasastan
Friendly enterprise

Friends Ciléne Andréhn and Marina Schiptjenko founded their gallery in 1991 after borrowing almost SEK24,000 from their parents then cycling around town until they chanced on a space. "When we started we wanted to work with artists of our own generation and, to a certain extent, this is still true," says Andréhn. "Some are still with us more than two decades on." The pair's plaudits include organising the inaugural Scandinavian outing of Frenchman Xavier Veilhan's colourful sculptural pieces.
2F, 8 Hudiksvallsgatan, 113 30
+46 (0)8 612 0075
andrehn-schiptjenko.com

② Galerie Forsblom, Vasastan
History repeating

Ebba Bozorgnia and Anna Persson unveiled this roomy gallery in 2017 with an excellent Ai Weiwei exhibition. The offshoot of Kaj Forsblom's renowned Helsinki gallery is a big arena that was given life by New York architect Richard Gluckman.

The rooms usually host three contemporary-art exhibitions that oscillate between better-known and obscure works. "One hundred years ago Stockholm's art scene was ahead of its time, showing Picasso at the same time as Paris; we're bringing that back," says Bozorgnia.
9 Karlavägen, 114 24
+46 (0)8 207 807
galerieforsblom.com

③ Galleri Magnus Karlsson, Norrmalm
Going solo

Supporting emerging Nordic artists is a shared cause in the city's top galleries and Magnus Karlsson is firmly at the apex of the movement. Among others it has showcased the macabre ceramic sculptures of Klara Kristalova and dark figurative paintings by Mamma Andersson.

The dozen or so exhibitions each year are dedicated almost exclusively to solo shows. Located beneath Stockholm's Royal Academy of Fine Arts, the gallery literally carries the weight of art on its shoulders – and carries it well.
12 Fredsgatan, 111 52
+46 (0)8 660 4353
gallerimagnuskarlsson.com

4

Bohman-Knäpper, Östermalm
International push

Lars Bohman sold his eponymous gallery in 2006 and 11 years later unveiled this space with Angelika Knäpper, the director of his former gallery. The new space opened with an exhibition of abstract canvases by New Yorker Jonathan Lasker, a choice indicative of the gallery's desire to push more international art in a city that's covetous of homegrown talent.

That's not to imply neglect for Scandinavia: you can often see the works of Norwegian Bjarne Melgaard with Swedes Lars Lerin and Marie-Louise Ekman.
36 Sturegatan, 114 36
+46 (0)8 289 793
bohman-knapper.com

Comic genius

Serie Galleriet is a quirky spot exhibiting illustrations from comic books by the genre's finest, and mostly Swedish, artists. You may not make sense of everything but language is never a barrier to appreciating a witty sketch. There's also a shop selling framed originals.
seriegalleriet.se

5

CFHill, Norrmalm
Art house

"We didn't want to be another white cube; we wanted to be inviting and exciting," says Michael Elmenbeck, CFHill's co-founder. And the gallery feels like a home, with three shows a month across its eight individually decorated spaces. The historic interiors enhance the impact of the contemporary art – an effect that's regularly captured in a comely printed catalogue.

Elmenbeck runs the space with Michael Storåkers and Anna-Karin Pusic *(all pictured, left to right)*. "We want to give something to Stockholm that it hasn't seen before," says Elmenbeck.
24 Norrlandsgatan, 111 43
cfhill.com

Live venues
Sounds good

1

Södra Teatern, Södermalm
A song at sunset

This grand old theatre in Södermalm is home to the most varied music events in the capital. The main stage hosts concerts from acoustic to a spot of indie rock. In the basement, behind a wrought-iron façade, is a former 19th-century bowling alley that now serves as grungy club Kägelbanan.

If it's warm head up to the Mosebacke terrace for the open-air concerts. The real gem is on the top floor: the champagne bar's smaller terrace offers some of the best views of Stockholm, especially during a rosy sunset.

1-3 Mosebacke Torg, 116 46
+46 (0)8 5319 9490
sodrateatern.com

2

Trädgården, Södermalm
Don't stop the party

During a typical summer weekend, 4,000 people head to Trädgården underneath Skanstullbron in Södermalm. It's popular with summer clubbers but its offering extends far beyond the nocturnal.

Since it opened in 2003 it has welcomed restaurants, an art gallery, bars, a cinema and a spot to play table tennis or pétanque. Sundays are busiest as crowds turn up for the flea market. There is a relaxed family vibe with live music in the day but at dusk things go up a peg or two at the Under Bron club, which is open until 03.00.

2 Hammarby Slussväg, 118 60
+46 (0)8 644 2023
tradgarden.com

3

Fasching, Norrmalm
Jazz it up

Bebop-lovers needn't venture far from Centralstation to appreciate crooning at the city's best jazz venue. Guests cram in shoulder to shoulder, as they have since it opened in 1977. Behind the neon sign is a dimly lit haunt with a mezzanine bar and restaurant that hosts a varied line-up, from hard bop to Swedish reggae.

Mondays are best if you want to give the tourists the slip: the night is an impromptu jam with no programme. Bolder audience members be mindful: the mic isn't up for grabs.

63 Kungsgatan, 111 22
+46 (0)8 200 066
fasching.se

④

Royal Swedish Opera, Norrmalm
Courting drama

When revellers arrived in 1792 for a royal ball at the opera, few anticipated the assassination of the opera's founder King Gustav III. The sad event led to the building being closed and later demolished.

Architect Axel Anderberg planned the new venue that opened on the same spot in 1889 and, while the peach-hued exterior is relatively restrained, the interiors are anything but. The stage, set beneath a beautiful painted ceiling, hosts performances that maintain a reverence for history without being afraid to go against the grain.
2 Gustav Adolfs torg, 103 22
+46 (0)8 791 4400
operan.se

⑤

Musikaliska, Norrmalm
Contrasting concerts

The hall's look may hark back to its construction in 1878 but the atmosphere is far from old hat. There are still classical repertoires among the 800 concerts each year, including those by the Stockholm County orchestra, as well as jazz, piano and choral events.

But drop by in the balmier months and you'll find a younger crowd spilling out onto the waterfront. Fridays and Saturdays host some of the best European DJs, who play well into the wee hours (in delightful contrast to the previous evening's black-tie bunch).
11 Nybrokajen, 111 48
+46 (0)8 5457 0300
musikaliska.se

Films
Timeless charm

①

Bio Rio, Södermalm
Salon service

This cinema recently received funding that helped architect Kristoffer Sundin preserve designer Albin Stark's neon-lit 1940s charm. From their plush red seats, patrons are treated to a variety of films – always played in their intended language and never dubbed – from Hollywood blockbusters to indie gems. It's a single-screen affair so what you gain in atmosphere you pay for in choice. The café on the ground floor serves good grub and if you'd like a glass of red wine and a cheese board during the film, ask for a spot at the salon at the back.
3 Hornstulls strand, 117 39
+46 (0)8 669 9500
biorio.se

2

Victoria, Södermalm
Veering towards experimental

The Victoria opened in 1936 and has been preserved masterfully, from the cursive sign above the entrance to the mermaid fountain in the foyer. The doors to the main auditorium also host marquetry that honours four cinematic trades: the actor, scriptwriter, director and cinematographer.

In 1973 the venue was expanded and today it has seven screens, the programmes of which often veer into the experimental: the Victoria screened Milos Forman's *One Flew over the Cuckoo's Nest* for 11 years without interruption from 1987.
67 Götgatan, 116 21
+46 (0)8 5626 0000
svenskabio.se

Stockholm on film

01 **Summer with Monika, 1953:** Stockholm forms the backdrop to most of Ingmar Bergman's early films. This one takes you to the archipelago with two working-class teenagers, who spend a few passionate months here before things change as the autumn chill arrives and it's time to return to the city.

02 **The Man on the Roof, 1977:** A classic that began the Beck franchise. The film is considered one of the finest thrillers about police brutality and corruption and has plenty of lofty aerial shots of central Stockholm.

03 **Let the Right One In, 2008:** This vampire horror thriller, set in the Stockholm suburb of Blackeberg in the 1980s, was Tomas Alfredson's international breakthrough as a director in 2009. A shy boy named Oskar falls in love with vampire-girl Eli, with chilling consequences.

04 **Easy Money, 2010:** A thriller set in Stockholm's underworld. Joel Kinnaman, who has since appeared in Netflix's *House of Cards*, plays JW, a student who gets involved with drug dealers to fund a lavish lifestyle.

05 **The Girl with the Dragon Tattoo, 2011:** In David Fincher's thriller, the second on-screen adaptation of the Swedish book, investigative reporter Mikael Blomkvist (Daniel Craig) and hacker Lisbeth Salander (Rooney Mara) become entangled in a web of corruption. Large parts of the movie were shot in Södermalm and Gamla Stan.

3
Zita Folkets Bio, Norrmalm
Avant garde old-timer

Built in 1913 by Georg Hagström and Frithiof Ekman, Zita is Stockholm's oldest cinema. Originally known as the Winter Palace and designed as a theatre, it switched to a cinema layout at the last minute and also served as a dance hall in the 1950s.

Despite its age, its bill is the most alternative in town: Tuesday evenings are dedicated to French cinema and there are also festivals devoted to countries or themes that might seem more at home in a gallery than a cinema.
37 Birger Jarlsgatan, 111 45
+46 (0)8 232 020
zita.se

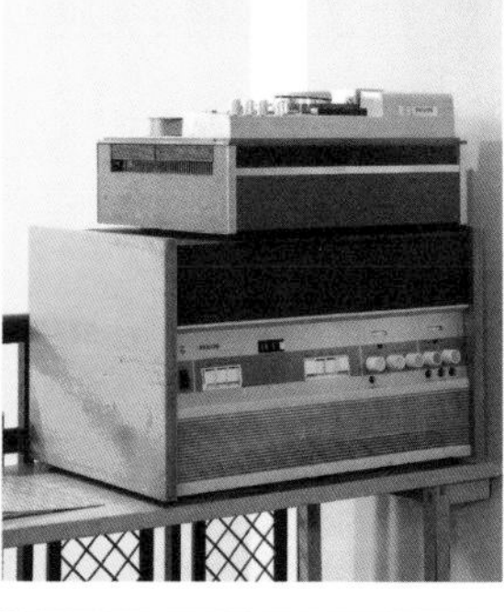

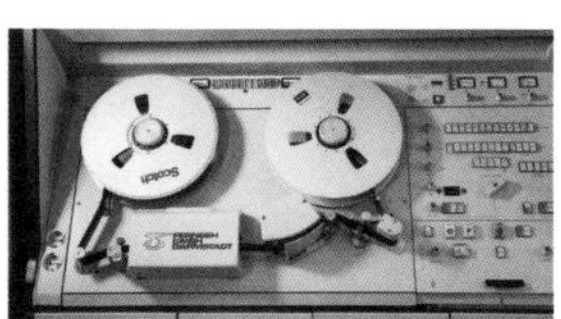

Media round-up
Into the mix

1
Media
Reading material

The free press has a proud history here (it clocked up 250 years in 2016) and so the gamut of opinions on most newsstands is heartening. Conservative daily ❶ *Svenska Dagbladet* is Sweden-focused, while the liberal-leaning and prestigious ❷ *Dagens Nyheter* casts its eye beyond the border. English-language biannual ❸ *Bon* leads the stack of magazines in women's fashion, with interviews, essays and photography that run from the avant garde to the plain gritty.

For a look at Sweden's enviable architecture, ❹ *Arkitektur* has been published eight times a year since 1901, while interior-design magazine ❺ *My Residence* launched in 2016. The latter's yearly issue peeks into some dozen homes across a chosen region and interviews the (understandably happy) residents, in English no less.

We've also found something colourful and fun for the nippers called ❻ *Koko*. Politically savvy weekly ❼ *Fokus* writes on current affairs and is Sweden's primary source for harder-hitting reports. ❽ *Arena* delivers a slightly lighter voice on politics and culture and comes out once every two months.

2
Pressbyrån, citywide
Read all about it

Lacklustre compared with the kiosk culture of Rome or Paris, Stockholm still has spots that stock the best of international and domestic print – you just need to know where to find them. Points of sale tend to be dominated by big chains rather than independents. Pressbyrån is the largest and stocks a wide selection, from art-house magazines such as *Folk* and *Bon* to international newspapers in most of the usual languages.

If you're in Södermalm you can also drop into Press Stop on Götgatan, which may prove fruitful for those in search of niche titles.
pressbyran.se

Stockholm's best Swedish-language radio

01 P4: Stockholm's public-service channel P4 is listened to by 300,000 Swedes a day. Keep updated on local news, with bulletins starting at 06.30. *Musikplats Stockholm* features live performances, with new Swedish artists on Fridays.
sverigesradio.se/stockholm

02 Värvet: In this podcast, Kristoffer Triumf meets musicians, writers, media figures and actors and grills them about politics, their dreams and work. *Värvet* is Swedish for "the task". There's also an English version called *Värvet International*.
värvet.se

03 Mix Megapol: The latest hits and oldies-but-goodies from Sweden and abroad, mixed with light chatter about a few less-pressing and more-parochial issues (only in Swedish, sadly, but the music's good). This is the channel to tune into before a night on the tiles. Try its morning programme if you're not in the mood for the harder-hitting news on the public service channels.
radioplay.se/mixmegapol

Do you really have to sing? Surely there are carols on the radio...

Design and architecture
The built environment

If Stockholm was a book then chapter one would be Gamla Stan: the hotchpotch of rusty-hued townhouses is an arresting prologue. But it's not the whole story. Yes there are the sky-splitting church spires and baroque palaces that betray the nation's royal lineage but there are also the cleaner lines and clipped look of Nordic classicism in many of the city's best buildings.

Modernism left its mark from the 1950s onwards, with the Kaknästornet TV tower, the Svenska Filmhuset and the odd (as in, both unusual and infrequent) reimagined church. Plus there are the advertisers – particularly those who lit up at the prospect of neon – and even a final resting place that celebrates rather than mourns its residents. Here are the design delights worth uncovering on your trip.

Contemporary
Here and now

(1)
Strandparken, Sundbyberg
Tree houses

These four timber apartment blocks are a little further out but worth the visit. They were designed by Wingårdh architects and realised by Folkhem, a Swedish developer that is planning 6,000 more living spaces in the capital.

The project, completed in 2012, is the first such high-rise in the city and Folkhem has sites for three new developments nearing approval. Part of a programme called Stockholm in Wood, the homes are made solely from timber; the pretty perches are coated in cedar shingles from Moelven Wood, so they're sustainable and nod to traditional Nordic architecture.
7-19 Hamngatan, 172 66

Stockholm Waterfront Congress Centre, Norrmalm
Sustainable structure

White Arkitekter completed this project in 2011. It belongs to the Rezidor Hotel Group, holds 3,000 guests and encompasses offices and a hotel tower. Encased by 21km of stainless-steel bars (giving it the nickname *Mälarkronan*, or "the Crown of Lake Mäkaren"), it's one of the world's most energy-efficient buildings: its glass façade comprises more than 1,000 sq m of solar collectors and the building is cooled with water from the lake. The woody interior is courtesy of RPW Design.
4 Nils Ericsons Plan, 111 64
+46 (0)8 5050 6000
stockholmwaterfront.com

Goodness, that building's HUGE! Oh, right, yes

③
KTH School of Architecture, Norra Djurgården
Quiet reflection

The new School of Architecture at Stockholm's Royal Institute of Technology (KTH) was a Tham & Videgård project completed in 2015. The cylindrical building, which is clad in red Corten steel, is well suited to the campus and has big windows that reflect its surroundings.
8 Brinellvägen, 114 28

Fair trade

The annual Stockholm Furniture & Light Fair takes place during the city's design week every February. The gathering of talent attracts tens of thousands of visitors seeking home and office additions.
stockholmfurniturelightfair.se; stockholmdesignweek.com

④

Stora Bryggeriet, Kungsholmen
Hop to it

Stockholm architecture firm Joliark transformed the abandoned Stora Bryggeriet brewery in western Kungsholmen, dating from 1890, into an office space for Swiss pharmaceutical company Octapharma. The façade was refurbished brick by brick and complemented with a large gabled glass front.

Its interior is characterised by high ceilings, which are adorned with exposed timber beams, and houses offices, conference rooms and a spacious cafeteria – in which beer sadly no longer flows freely.
23 Lars Forssells gata, 112 51
+46 (0)8 5664 3000
joliark.se

Going green

In 2010 Stockholm received the European Green Capital award and became Europe's first nominated "environmental capital". The city is so effective at dealing with waste that it has been known to buy more from neighbours to keep its plants running.

⑤

Ericsson Globe, Johanneshov
You shall go to the ball

The Ericsson Globe, opened in 1989, was designed by Berg Arkitektkontor and is the world's largest spherical building, with a diameter of some 110 metres. Situated in the fittingly named Globe City, it can be seen from miles away.

The arena seats more than 16,000 for concerts and about 14,000 for sporting events, particularly ice hockey. In 2009, Swedish telecoms firm Ericsson bought the rights to its name from Stockholm Globe Arena and introduced a circular glass-encased gondola, known as Skyview, to explore the futuristic structure.
Globe City, 121 77
+46 (0)8 600 9100

⑥

Ferry terminal, Norrmalm
Harbour intent

Stockholm's harbour is a great spot from which to glimpse some of the city's best landmarks. And despite being new additions, Strömkajen's contemporary ferry terminals fit right in.

Set on the promenade opposite Gamla Stan, the three geometric terminal buildings by Marge Arkitekter provide a pretty gateway to Stockholm's archipelago. Each uses tiles of burnished Tombak (a brass alloy), while doorways and windows act as mirrors and reflect the Royal Palace, National Art Gallery and the bobbing boats and rippling bay beyond. A triumph of new ideas in an age-old setting.
Stockholm Strömkajen, 111 48

Postwar
Boom years

1

Svenska Filmhuset, Östermalm
Scene setter

Architect Peter Celsing designed the home of the Swedish Film Institute in 1970. "No ordinary bloody building," is what institute founder Harry Schein is said to have asked for; he wasn't disappointed.

The brutalist structure lies north of the Gärdet plain and features two screening rooms – Victor (364 seats) and Mauritz (130 seats) – as well as a restaurant and a library devoted to literature on film. The entire place is shaped like a camera and the rectangular windows were designed to resemble the perforated edge of film.

The neon-lit Bauhaus-style lettering on the exterior is a nod to the golden age of Hollywood and the long incline that leads to the entrance, ahem, ramps up the expectation as you enter. The interior was recently revamped by AIX Arkitekter.

1-5 Borgvägen, 115 53
+46 (0)8 665 1100
filminstitutet.se

②

Riksbanken, Norrmalm

Give credit

The Bank of Sweden is one of postwar maestro Peter Celsing's best-known buildings; finished in 1976, it took six years to build. Deep-set windows punctuate the impregnable-looking granite façade and it's crowned with a glass-and-copper penthouse.

The interior is light and bright, the ceiling, walls and furniture made from birch sourced in northern Sweden and Finland. Geometric shapes are the hallmarks, from the circular meeting room to the rectangular courtyard, while art by Ulrik Samuelson, Sivert Lindblom and Olle Nyman completes the look.

11 Brunkebergstorg, 111 51
+46 (0)8 787 0000

③

Pa Soder Crescent, Södermalm

Post-modern playground

Barcelona-born Ricardo Bofill's contribution to Stockholm seems almost tame compared to other buildings he's worked on. The concrete structure is a rare monument to post-modern architecture, a playful pastiche of styles from the classical to the, frankly, bonkers.

The complex was built on the site of a former railyard in 1992 and holds 310 apartments. If you're struggling to locate the crescent monument then look out for Dane Henning Larsen's equally incongruous-looking 40-floor lantern-like tower block, which abuts Bofill's yellow creation.

Södermalmsallén, 118 27

④

Hötorgsskraporna, Norrmalm

Famous five

This quintet of 18-storey office towers (or, as they were dubbed by planning commissioner Yngve Larsson, "five trumpet blasts") were completed between 1955 and 1966, marking what was intended as the city's new commercial centre.

David Helldén, Anders Tengbom, Sven Markelius, LE Lallerstedt and Backström & Reinius created the buildings, which are lined up like dominos as part of a city plan by Markelius. The area didn't live up to expectations but a renewal programme in the 1990s ensured that the towers (and Olle Baertling's mural on tower one) remained intact.

1-17 Seavägen, 111 57

⑤

Markuskyrkan, Björkhagen

Saintly presence

Historic church spires feature heavily in the city's skyline yet, believe it or not, Sweden's greatest church-building era didn't set in until the 1960s. This is when architect Sigurd Lewerentz's Markuskyrkan in Björkhagen, a suburb south of Stockholm, was completed.

The brutalist structure – with its cubic dark-brick façade, reminiscent of a bunker, and subtle detailing – is Lewerentz's most noted building and was awarded the first Kasper Salin Prize in 1962.

51 Malmövägen, 121 53 Johanneshov
svenskakyrkan.se

Bonnierhuset, Norrmalm

Column inches

Anders and Ivar Tengbom designed this biscuit-coloured number for publisher Bonnier in 1939 and it was completed a decade later. Located between Torsgatan and the railroad tracks on the bank of Barnhusviken Canal, the brick building sought to offer density in height to downtown Norrmalm.

The tower originally housed editorial offices, while the lower floors facing the railway were home to the printers and distributors. In 2006, Johan Celsing Arkitektkontor extended it with an art gallery, its glass-and-steel façade marking the break with the older and statelier original structure.

21 Torsgatan, 113 21

⑦

Kaknästornet, Ladugårdsgärdet
Height of good taste

This rocket-like structure is invariably visible out of the corner of your eye. Designed by architects Hans Borgström and Bengt Lindroos, it was unveiled in 1967 as a telecom tower and still serves that purpose, responsible for most ingoing and outgoing TV signals.

Stockholmers didn't warm to the tower initially, considering it an eyesore for decades until a newfound nostalgia for mid-century design mollified their formerly entrenched opinions. If you get a chance to climb it, the vista from the top is perhaps the city's finest.

28-30 Mörka Kroken, 115 27
+46 (0)8 667 2180
kaknastornet.se

Early 20th century
Burgeoning infrastructure

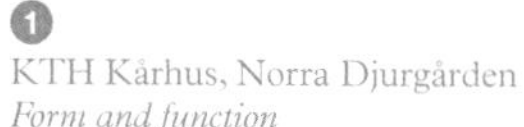

❶

KTH Kårhus, Norra Djurgården
Form and function

Kårhuset Nymble, the student union at the Royal Institute of Technology, is one of the city's best functionalist buildings (think straight lines and concrete). Designed by Sven Markelius and Uno Åhrén in 1928 and completed in 1930, the Bauhaus-style building forms an L-shape around a courtyard.

Steps lead up to the entrance and inside to the clubroom and library. On the middle level is a light-flooded dining hall. The building has been expanded twice by Sven Markelius and Bengt Lindroos of Kaknästornet fame (*pictured, left*) and was fully restored in 1999.

15-19 Drottning Kristinas väg, 100 44
ths.kth.se

②

Stadshuset, Kungsholmen
Nobel undertaking

City hall is an example of national romanticism, although architect Ragnar Östberg drew on Italian renaissance designs. Completed in the 1920s, it's formed around two "piazzas": the exterior courtyard and the Blue Hall, where the Nobel Banquet is held. (Östberg planned to paint the hall blue but opted against it – though the name stuck.)

The Golden Hall does live up to its name, clad in Einar Forseth's Byzantine-inspired mosaic of 18 million pieces of gold and glass. It depicts Sweden's history from the 9th century.

1 Hantverkargatan, 111 52
+46 (0)8 5082 9058
stockholm.se

③
Skurubron, Nacka
Novel crossing

When it was built in 1915, Lars Israel Wahlman's Skurubron was already a daring affair – particularly as it was made of concrete. Spanning 280 metres in length, it was praised upon completion and a second bridge added in parallel in 1957.

Yet that wasn't enough to accommodate the 52,000 commuters heading into Stockholm every day so Dissing + Weitling were selected to design an additional bridge, for which construction began in 2015. It will work in tandem with the historical Skurubron and is designed to complement the landmark with a subtle steel deck.
222 Våg, Skuruborn

Into the woods
—
The Skogskyrkogården (woodland cemetery) in Enskededalen took a quarter of a century to build and is a high-water mark of modernism. Designed by Swedish architects Gunnar Asplund and Sigurd Lewerentz, it reflects the development from Nordic classicism.

④
Kungstornen, Norrmalm
The two towers

Considered by some to be Europe's first skyscrapers and conceived in 1919 by architect Sven Wallander, the 60-metre-tall King's Towers were completed between 1924 and 1925. Wallander's design for the north tower was inspired by US architect Louis Sullivan, the "father of skyscrapers". The south tower was created by Ivar Callmander.
28-33 Kungsgatan, 111 35

⑤
Konserthuset, Norrmalm
Democratic principles

Ivar Tengbom's mid-1920s building draws on Athens for its tall columns and was among the city's first major venues not to have separate entrances based on social class.

The imposing main façade is marked by 10 columns and a fountain made up of bronze figures playing instruments (it's called the "Orpheus Group" and was designed by Carl Milles). In the main foyer you'll find four more statues by Milles – depicting four Muses – as well as mosaics by Einar Forseth and furniture by Carl Malmsten. The music isn't bad either.
8 Hötorget, 103 87
+46 (0)8 786 0200
konserthuset.se

STOCKHOLMS STADSBIBLIOT
ARKITEKT GUNNAR ASPLUND

Kopiering
Copying

STOCKHOLM PUBLIC LIBRARY
ARCHITECT GUNNAR ASPLUND 1928

Open book
—
Inside and out, the library is bright and welcoming

⑥
Stadsbibliotek, Vasastan
Read all about it

This sprightly orange pantheon to knowledge became one of the leading examples of Swedish grace architecture. Gunnar Asplund was initially tasked with commissioning an architect for the structure but was handed the contract outright after city hall saw his ideas.

Asplund opted for an almost austere, cylindrical blueprint so that the architecture wouldn't dominate the building's contents. But look closely and you'll find neoclassical ornamentations that contrast with the simplicity, such as the Graeco-Egyptian frieze around the exterior.

73 Sveavägen, 113 50
+46 (0)8 5083 1100
bibliotek.stockholm.se

7

Centralposten, Normalm
Alpha mail

Architect Ferdinand Boberg's vast art nouveau building takes up a whole city block and was the post office headquarters from 1903 to 2003. The turret-flanked red-brick affair features rows of windows and soft stone ornaments symbolising the industry; look out for post horns and carrier pigeons.

The main entrance sits below a domed clock tower; step inside and you'll find a vaulted cupola and sandstone floors that match the red hue of the exterior. The building was declared a historical monument in 1935 and has undergone several renovations since, the latest in 2008 under Ahrbom & Partner.
28-34 Vasagatan, 111 20

Notable Swedish architects

01 Erik Gunnar Asplund (1885-1940): Asplund made a name for himself between the wars as a leading proponent of 1920s neoclassicism and a pioneer of functionalism (boxes and straight lines for the most part). Over his lifetime he completed more than 40 projects, mostly public buildings, such as Skogskyrkogården's Woodland Chapel and Crematorium, the Stockholm Public Library and the Skandia Cinema.

02 Sigurd Lewerentz (1885-1975): One of Sweden's best-loved architects, Lewerentz designed pavilions at the Stockholm Exhibition of 1930. His most celebrated piece of work in the city is the dark-brick and light-mortar Markuskyrkan (*see page 111*), understated but beautiful in the shadow of a copse of birch trees in Björkhagen.

03 Sven Markelius (1889-1972): A forerunner of Swedish functionalism, Markelius was also one of the country's leading modernists and played a big role in shaping postwar Stockholm. Inspired by Le Corbusier, he left a sizeable legacy, including the modernist manifesto *Acceptera*. Before becoming head of the Stockholm planning office between 1944 and 1954 he was involved in many high-profile developments in the city, including Hötorgsskraporna (*see page 111*) and designing the urban plan for Vällingby. Other Stockholm projects include Villa Markelius and Villa Myrdal.

Traditional
Established classics

Nordiska Museet, Djurgården
Statement of values

The Nordic Museum is a retort to the industrialisation of 19th-century Sweden. Architect Isak Gustaf Clason chose the style of the Swedish-Danish renaissance for the castle's design, which went up in 1907. The lofty main hall features a limestone floor studded with symbols of the elements and minerals uncovered by Swedish chemist Torbern Bergman.
6-16 Djurgårdsvägen, 115 93
+46 (0)8 5195 4600
nordiskamuseet.se

(2)

Riksdagshuset, Helgeandsholmen
Housing of Parliament

Aron Johansson's parliament house was built in 1905. The neoclassical complex, with its Corinthian-style columns, is most impressive when you enter via the archway on Riksgatan, just past the Riksbron.

On your left is the parliament itself and on the right the former Bank of Sweden. The two buildings were brought together in the 1980s and architecture firm AOS added a glass-gallery extension with views of the Riddarfjärden to the former bank, which now houses the parliament's main entrance.

1 Riksgatan, 100 12
+46 (0)8 786 4000
riksdagen.se

(3)

Kronobageriet, Östermalm
Rising fortunes

Stockholm's oldest industrial building was established in the 17th century. The bakery (and storage house, later to stock ammunition and weapons) supplied bread and buns to the town until 1958.

The building's thick, white exterior walls are adorned with wood-shuttered windows, iron anchor plates and brick corner quoins that show its age compared to Östermalm's characteristic art nouveau buildings. In the late 1970s architect Kjell Abramson converted it into a museum; it recently reopened as the Swedish Museum of the Performing Arts.
2 Sibyllegatan, 114 51
scenkonstmuseet.se

⑤

Dramaten, Östermalm

Top performer

King Gustav III established the national theatre, which now calls this art nouveau number home. Built in 1908 by Fredrik Lilljekvist, its Ekeberg marble façade bears a frieze of the festival of Dionysus (the Greek god of wine and frivolity) and flanking the entrance are gilded statues by John Börjeson.

On the western corner there's a bronze statue of Swedish actress Margaret Krook, designed by sculptor Marie-Louise Ekman. It's creepily realistic and heated to body temperature; rubbing its belly brings luck.

Nybroplan, 111 47
+46 (0)8 667 0680
dramaten.se

6

Old town, Gamla Stan

Middle Age marvel

Gamla Stan is one of the best-preserved medieval city centres in Europe. It also marks the place from which Sweden's capital has grown since it was founded in 1252.

The Old Town's labyrinthine streets feature small, decoratively gabled houses in sunny shades of yellow, orange and red. Within the former city walls stand the baroque-style cathedral Storkyrkan and the Börshuset. The latter, built in 1778, was Stockholm's stock exchange; now it's a museum dedicated to the winners of the Nobel prize. The biggest landmark in the district is the Royal Palace, designed by Nicodemus Tessin the Younger in 1754.

Leisure destinations
Great escapes

①
Hammarby Sjöstad Observatorium, Hammarby
Water feature

This pier, hewn from Canadian oak by Gunilla Bandolin, sits on stilts in the calm waters of Hammarby Sjö. The circular structure, in the rough likeness of a coiled seashell, is made up of curved benches that offer 360-degree views and has become a calm gathering point in a rapidly developing part of the city.

"I was interested in making a work of art that people could use," says Bandolin. In spring and summer "the cake" – as it's known locally – is a popular spot for picnics, performances and sunbathers, and even the odd wedding or christening.
Sickla Udde, 120 67

Hornsbergs Strandpark, Stadshagen
Liquid refreshment

The Beach Park in northwest Kungsholmen won the Swedish landscape award Sienapriset in 2012 for good reasons: Nyréns Architects successfully reconnected the residential neighbourhood with the lake and transformed the waterfront along Ulvsundasjön into an outdoor oasis, complete with three floating docks.

A meandering path leads through the 700-metre-long park, which has been planted with exotic flora and is interspersed with benches and barbecue spots. It's a prime perch for catching the sunset.
41 Hornsbergs Strand, 112 16

③
Skandia, Norrmalm
Screen time

In 1923 Gunnar Asplund, who was behind the public library (*see page 114*), created this cinema using Athenian-style caryatids (pillars carved to look like female figures) that support the upper circle, plus 60 silk-covered star-shaped lamps.

Today it hosts press screenings but architectural admirers are always welcome. The red neon signs and classical friezes lining the walls are still in place.
82 Drottninggatan, 111 36
+46 (0)8 5626 0000
sf.se

Metro stations
Underground galleries

01 02

What lies beneath

Stockholm's metro is an ever-evolving art gallery: more than 90 of its 100 stations have been decorated. The government launched the initiative in the 1950s to bring art to the people and, while similar projects saw light in Soviet Moscow, Stockholm preferred to grant its artists liberty rather than confine their work to propaganda.

(Pictures 01 to 02) Skarpnäck: Brooklyn-born artist Richard Nonas placed 17 granite seats along the platform in the 1990s. The red-brick flooring mimics the housing common to the Skarpnäck neighbourhood.
(03) Solna: Painted in 1975 by Swedes Anders Åberg and Karl-Olav Bjork, the red ceiling clashes with a 1km-long green mural of spruce trees: a warning against deforestation and rural depopulation.
(04) Östermalmstorg: Decked out in the 1960s by Siri Derkert with charcoal drawings of history's most prominent women, from ancient Greek mathematician Hypatia to British writer Virginia Woolf.
(05 to 06) T-Centralen: To honour the labourers who built T-Centralen Station in the 1970s, Per Olof Ultvedt painted their silhouettes along the cheerful white-and-blue walls.

03 04

05

06

Visual identity
Style of the city

①
Anchor plates
Holding patterns

These iron adornments, known as *ankarjärnslut*, are ubiquitous on Stockholm's older buildings. Until the 19th century, such tie-rods were used to hold structures in place, which is why they're commonly found in Gamla Stan.

They're everywhere once you notice them and offer clues as to when the buildings that they adorn were constructed. The oldest plates resemble hammer heads and date from the 16th century; in the 17th century they took the form of antlers; and by the 18th century they began to look like nooses (after short-lived incarnations as, variously, four-leaf clovers or the occasional spear).

Manhole covers
The hole story

If lore is to be believed, the fate of a person's love life can rest on these crested plates. Covers marked with a K, which stands for *källvatten* (fresh water), bring *kärlek* (love) to those who tread upon them. Those with an A for *avlopp* (sewage) bring worse fortunes. If you accidentally step on a sewer plate, three unsolicited pats on the back are said to reverse the bad luck.

Neon signs
Light entertainment

Neon signs touting everything from cinemas to shops have been a Stockholm fixture for nearly a century. From the revolving roundel atop the NK department store to the cursive script adorning Södermalm's Victoria cinema, many signs remain beloved hallmarks of the city's venerable institutions. A particularly eye-catching example is the Stomatol advertisement, erected in 1909. Sweden's first animated ad display (giving the illusion of toothpaste snaking onto an enormous brush) still lights up the sky above Slussenområdet. Stomatol may be long gone but sometimes a decent ad can stay fresher than the brand.

④
Spires
Steeple chasing

Storkyrkan in Gamla Stan is the city's oldest spire, dating from about 1280. Just south of it you'll find Tyska kyrkan, the German Church of Saint Gertrude, which documents Stockholm's long relationship with Germany. Yet neither of these come close to Riddarholmskyrkan: the city's only medieval abbey is the burial place of more than three centuries of Swedish royalty. Its spire was destroyed by lightning in 1835 and replaced with a filigree cast-iron one that has become a landmark in its own right.

Part of the plan

Stockholm's City Planning Department has its hands full to meet the demands of a city set to reach a population of one million by 2022. Luckily a dedicated Beauty Council ensures that new builds don't overshadow or clash with the existing architecture.

Sport and fitness
On the move

Water forms an integral part of life in the city (unsurprisingly, given that it's made up of a group of islands). As soon as the sun's out, locals hit the sandy inner-city beaches or take to the water on kayaks and plot a course for one of the archipelago's more remote fringes. If you'd rather observe the glittering Baltic from land, however, there are coastal cycle paths or runs aplenty – perhaps a trot around the perimeter of Djurgården, finishing with a tipple at Berzelii Park? (You've earned it.)

During cooler months there are many spots for working-out indoors. Stockholmers love a sauna and there are beautiful wood-panelled places scattered around town (the best, Yasuragi, takes inspiration from the Japanese tradition and is out east). 'Holmers are also a well-kempt bunch, tended by Södermalm barbers and Vasastan hairdressers. Read on for the capital's best places to get your heart rate racing and your coiffure suitably coiffed.

On the water
Wet, wet, wet

(1)
City beaches
Dip in

When it's hot, head to the city's sandy fringes. The best and most accessible spot is Långholmen, a large island northwest of Södermalm that's dotted with summer cottages and jetties. Head to its north coast (just behind the Långholmen Hotel, a former prison) and throw down a towel – just don't expect to be alone.

To the north of the city, a five-minute walk from Stockholm University and the Universitetet metro, you'll find Lake Brunnsviken. Its shores are ideal if you're after some solace (the students are away for much of the summer). Most visitors opt for Brunnsviksbadet Beach but there are plenty of other spots to discover.

To truly escape, take a 25-minute ferry from Nybroplan to Fjäderholmarna, a group of islands. Here it's all about cliff diving and perching on rocks but the azure waters and surrounding woodland make up for the lack of sand.

2

Kayaking

Paddle power

Swedes, on the whole, love a little sport in the water and kayaking is an agreeable way to see the city from a new perspective. Companies such as Stockholm Adventures offer two-hour guided tours around the harbour in two-seaters, starting at Djurgårdsbron, the bridge connecting Östermalm and Djurgården.

If you're feeling lazy, however, fear not. The many islands prevent stronger currents or riptides from holding sway or swell, meaning paddlers can enjoy smooth sailing all round. It's worth heading out to the archipelago too. The pristine waters surrounding the island of Runmarö, an hour-long ferry ride from the capital, are a popular destination for day-long kayaking trips. The hardier can opt for a three-day jaunt, complete with camping on the remote isle.

21 Kungsbro Strand, 112 26
+46 (0)8 336 001
stockholmadventures.com

Set sail

Come summer, Stockholm's archipelago (comprising some 30,000 islands) is dotted with white sailboats. This stretch of the Baltic is a good place for novices to learn – winds aren't too strong and tides are minimal – and companies such as Nautilus will kit you out. *nautilusyachting.com*

New horizons

Get a fresh perspective of the city in a kayak

Island day trips

The glorious archipelago is best experienced in the summer and its closest point is just a 30-minute trip from the city centre. Hop on a boat from Nybroplan and head to the Fjäderholmarna Islands. There's plenty to see and do: sunbathe on the cliffs, take a dip (of course), visit the glass-blowers' and pottery-makers' ateliers and enjoy a bite to eat at the Rökeriet restaurant.

Grinda can be reached in about an hour via the fastest boat. A lush natural reserve with secluded sandy beaches, this is one of Stockholm's best swimming spots. For a tasty meal or an overnight stay, check out Grinda Wärdshus inn, a pretty art nouveau building perched on a small hill.

For a longer trip we recommend Sandhamn or Utö, sometimes referred to as the Stureplan and Södermalm of the archipelago, respectively, for their busyness. Picturesque Sandhamn boasts a marina, small shops, bars, restaurants and hotels, as well as a sandy beach called Trouville and quiet forests. Utö, in the outer southern archipelago, attracts visitors year-round with the popular Utö Värdshus hotel and restaurant but its beaches are its best asset. Rent a bike and find your own.

All aboard! We're sailing to Sandhamn

Grooming
Cut-off points

Roy & Son, Södermalm
Trimming up

Peter Mannerstål is following in barber father Roy's footsteps. His salon is a classic affair with plush leather seats and colourful bottles of oils, balms and tinctures.

Need a beard trim? The most intricate option is the Knivsöder treatment, which includes several stages of hot and cold towels, preparatory oils and two shaves. Great unless you're in a hurry.
24 Hornsbruksgatan, 117 34
+46 (0)08 220 021
royandson.com

②
Barber & Books, Södermalm
Novel styles

After visiting a New York shop that combined haircuts with books, husband and wife Håkan and Catarina Ström, a barber and writer respectively, decided to do the same in Södermalm.

At the front of their space, decked out in red-and-white-checked tiles, the shelves are lined with art and photography books; at the back, Håkan trims the manes and beards of Stockholm's most dapper chaps, finishing things off with his in-house line of "Made in Sweden" grooming products.
21 Östgötagatan, 116 25
+46 (0)8 640 0227
barberandbooks.se

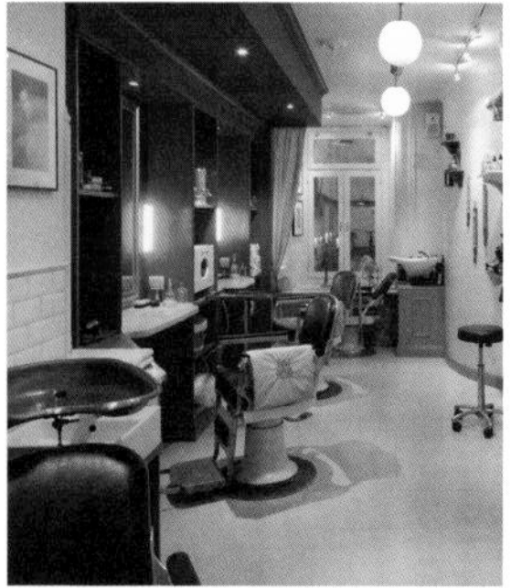

Koivisto Karlsson, Vasastan
Cut to the chase

With its avant garde work regularly featured atop the heads of purse-lipped models or in the pages of glossy magazines, Koivisto Karlsson is the spot for women after a new 'do (or a refresh of an old one).

Opened in 2007 by hair-colouring whizz Teemu Koivisto and Jenny Karlsson, who's all about the cutting and styling, the inner-city salon is a sleek affair: its vast white walls are decorated with black-and-white photographs and clients perch on natty black swivel chairs.
12 Tegnérgatan, 113 58
+46 (0)8 303 005
koivistokarlsson.se

Three gyms

01 Becore, Vasastan: This chic centre offers classes for barre, spinning and Lagree (a take on Pilates). Working out is easier in a space that looks this good, with its concrete or wood-panelled floors and forest-green walls. Classes cost SEK260 a pop; there is also a studio in Östermalm.
becore.se/studios/93

02 CrossFit Nordic, Vasastan: CrossFit, the exercise phenomenon involving high-intensity activities such as weightlifting and climbing, has made its way into Stockholm's gyms. Here you have a choice of three daily classes of varying degrees of difficulty. If you want to do your own thing there are plenty of weights and exercise bikes. Single passes cost SEK250.
crossfitnordic.se

03 Metropolis Gym, Östermalm: Run by Per Althini, Metropolis has all the trappings, with Technogym weights and machines downstairs, plus a yoga studio up top. A day pass costs SEK250.
metropolisgym.se

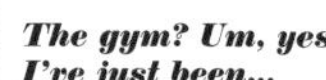

Spas
Rest and relaxation

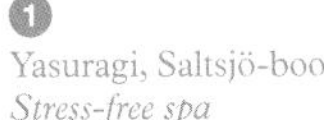

Yasuragi, Saltsjö-boo
Stress-free spa

Stockholm isn't a stressful city but it's still comforting to know that hotel and onsen Yasuragi is just 30 minutes away. The Yoji Kasajima-designed building has 191 rooms, all looking onto the archipelago.

Patrons must don a *yukata* (cotton gown) and can either stay the night in a traditional room complete with tatami mats (the suites even have their own hot springs) or drop in for a day at the baths and enjoy treatments such as charcoal massages or the sauna yoga. Technophobes rejoice: the spas also have a "digital silence" zone.
6 Hamndalsvägen, Saltsjö-Boo, 132 81
+46 (0)8 747 6100
yasuragi.se

Three more spas

01 **Sturebadet, Östermalm:** An art nouveau pool, sauna and massage parlour that dates back to 1885, Sturebadet's marble and dark-wood decor echoes the decadence of Ottoman baths. *sturebadet.se*

02 **Njuta Spa, Nacka Strand:** Although it's a little out of town, this charming country house is worth the trip. You can lounge in a jacuzzi overlooking the archipelago before sweltering in the sauna and the hosts will ply you with fresh fruit and champagne. *njutaspa.se*

03 **Nordic Spa at Grand Hôtel, Norrmalm:** This hotel offers a range of packages but we recommend the Head Start: a shoulder massage is followed by trips to the pool and sauna before you are treated to breakfast. *grandhotel.se*

Cycling routes
In the frame

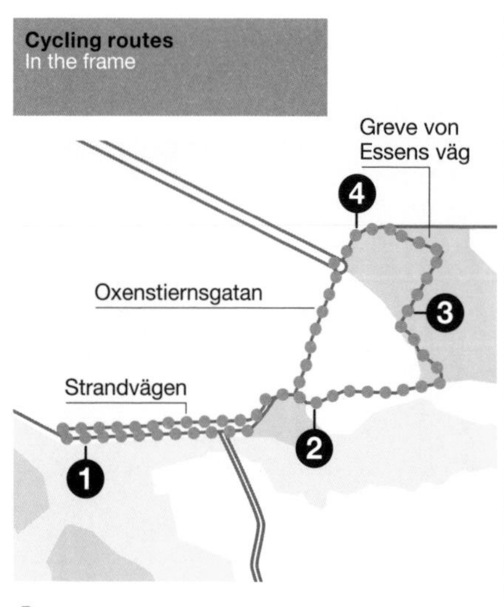

① Östermalm
Easy rider

A leisurely cycle through Östermalm, neighbouring Embassy Village and Ladugårdsgärdet Park.

STARTING POINT: Strandvägen in Östermalm
DISTANCE: 5km

Grab your wheels at ❶ *Rent-a-Bike* at 18 Strandvägen and head east down the boulevard. Continue past Djurgårdsbron as the road curves left and inclines, then past the 1970s ❷ *Berwaldhallen* concert hall. Keep left as the road splits, turning onto Dag Hammarskjölds väg. The stretch ahead has a cluster of embassies, the first on the left being that of the US. Speed past the tree-lined stretch to the expansive Ladugårdsgärdet Park, just after the modernist and ivy-covered gem of the Norwegian embassy.

Take the first left into the park and cycle for some 300 metres, taking the second right and dipping into the park. To your right is the brutalist ❸ *Kaknastörnet TV tower*, a once-controversial affair that's become an unlikely city icon and houses a top-floor restaurant. Continue to Greve von Essens väg, turning left and continuing to the traffic lights, then turn left again. Ahead and slightly to the right is the peerless ❹ *Svenska Filmhuset*, its windows designed to resemble perforated rolls of camera film.

Follow the road as it curves into the grander residential quarters of Östermalm. Cross over the roundabout and continue, with the pink-hued building of Stockholm's University of the Arts on your right. You'll soon hit the Nobelparken and the Berwaldhallen again. Turn right at the T-junction then it's down the slope and back towards Strandvägen. Drop your bike off where you started or continue into the heart of the city for a little more adventure.

❷ Hagaparken
Bespoked travel

Explore a glorious park with lots of royal history and architectural oddities.

STARTING POINT: Narvavägen in Östermalm
DISTANCE: Round-trip is 9km of city cycling, plus a couple more through the park

You can grab a simple City Bike from street locations all over Stockholm but for something with a bit more oomph hire a Bianchi or DBS from Bike Sweden at 17 Narvavägen. Head north to ❶ *Karlaplan* at the end of the block. This mini park, where several boulevards meet, feels a bit like Rome on sunny days when the fountain is at full throttle.

Continue west along elegant Karlavägen, which leads into Birger Jarlsgatan after 2km. As you merge left into Valhallavägen the roads become slightly less charming – but don't lose heart. At the ring road take the first exit and then turn right at the designated cycling path; between the trees you'll see a small dirt track. This takes you along the western edge of Bellevue Park (where you can visit the ❷ *Carl Eldh Studio Museum*) and out onto Brunnsviksvägen. Turn left and continue to the crossroads, just after a restaurant.

Go right and continue along the waterfront until you enter ❸ *Hagaparken*. It's worth the effort: Haga is designed in the classic English style around a huge lake, Brunnsviken. It's long been associated with the royal family, who built all sorts of curiosities here over the centuries, such as the 1787 Chinese Pavilion and the ❹ *1788 Turkish Pavilion*. Once in the park there are many routes to follow. You can venture deep into the woodland or simply loop around the pavilion (an orange structure decorated with blue stars) and head back towards Bike Sweden.

Running routes
On the right track

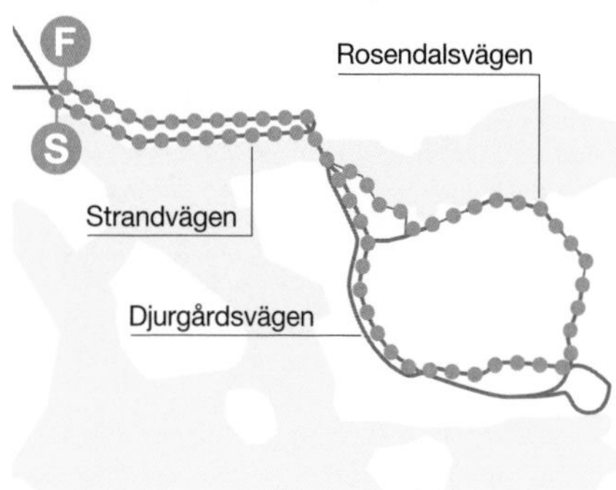

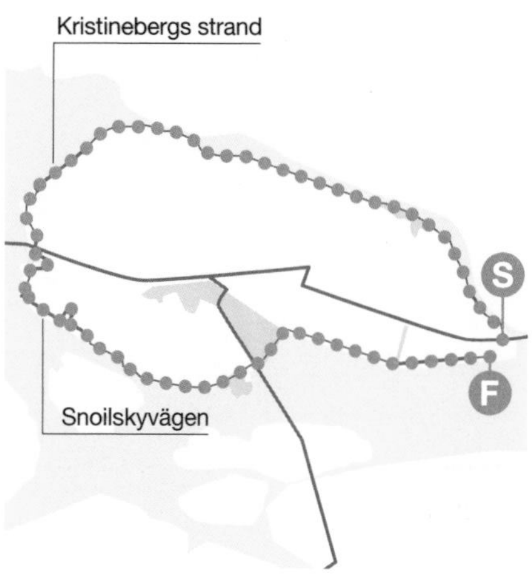

Djurgården
Building tour

DISTANCE: 5.4km
GRADIENT: Gentle inclines
DIFFICULTY: Easy
HIGHLIGHT: Glimmering waterfront and woodland with architectural spirit-lifters throughout
BEST TIME: Late afternoon
NEAREST METRO: Östermalmstorg

Start on Strandvägen at the northern tip of Berzelii Park. Head southeast along the water (closest to the buildings) to a crossroads. Cross Djurgårdsbron (the bridge on your right) and zip left through the *Blå Porten* (Blue Gates) erected by King Oscar I, whose monogram is on top. Stay by the water; through the trees to the right is old merchant's mansion *Lusthusporten*.

At the fourth fork in the road go right towards Wårdshuset Ulla Winbladh and then, at the crossroads, left onto Rosendalsvägen. Things get steeper now. Stay right as the road splits; the orange-yellow building with the tower on the right is a former exhibition pavilion by *Gustaf Wickman*. At the crossing go right onto Sirishovsvägen, then right again at the next one. The road meets the tram-lined Djurgårdsvägen but turn right before that onto Singlebacken, then stay in the middle lane (it splits into three).

After a while the path slopes back down to the aforementioned Djurgårdsvägen; turn right and follow it as it curves right. You'll pass the orange-walled *Liljevalchs Konsthall* gallery on your left and a pillar topped by Carl Milles' 1919 statue "Archer". Pass the *Nordiska Museet* on the left and cross Djurgårdsbron back to Östermalm. The first statue on the right, atop the bridge, is Norse god Thor. Turn left back onto Strandvägen, keeping close to the water, and finish at Berzelii Park.

Kungsholmen
Waterfront wonder

DISTANCE: Up to 9km
GRADIENT: Cross-country dips, one cliff-side scramble
DIFFICULTY: Easy (apart from a rocky stretch)
HIGHLIGHT: Seeing how locals spend sunny days
BEST TIME: Mid-morning
NEAREST METRO: Centralstation or Rådhuset

Start at the eastern point of *Hantverkargatan* with your back to city hall. Run north to the water and follow the path as it veers west. It's shared with cyclists but, except in rush hour, it's not too busy. You'll pass under four bridges. After about 2.5km you'll see Karlberg Palace across the water, which was built in 1630 and is now a military academy. Keep going straight and, on your left you'll pass a *koloniträdgård*: a collection of cabins with flower-filled gardens.

Next you'll come to *Stadshagen*, a waterfront development that entices Swedes on summer days (and nights). The path leads past a harbour, up a wooden staircase and into woodland. Now come steep slopes and sharp dips and after 2km you'll see a grey-and-white building on your right: this is *Fredhälls Badklubb*, where locals swim.

Now you have a choice: stick to the road or continue across the cliffs. For the cliffs, go straight on at the Badklubb. It's a narrow path with a metal handrail for support and a fun (and safe) scramble. For the road, scoot up the stairs to Snoilskyvägen and follow it along, keeping the water on your right. Cross through the small park and continue on Atterbomsvägen. When you reach Scheffersgatan take the path on your right. It will lead you down to *Smedsuddsbadet*, a popular beach, then a park, *Rålambshovsparken*, and the long, level stretch along Norr Mälarstrand back to city hall.

Walks
— Wander this way

The nature-loving Swedes have long designed Stockholm with walkers in mind – even if Gamla Stan's cobbles are a little tricky to traverse. Here we'll take you on a tour of all the main neighbourhoods, from grid-charted Vasastan to gritty Södermalm (our only omission is Djurgården to the east, which we suggest you save for a sunny cycle or run). So get that coffee to go: we have a whole city to explore.

NEIGHBOURHOOD 01

Gamla Stan and Norrmalm
Splendid heritage

Despite being separated by just a thin strip of water, Gamla Stan (Old Town) and Norrmalm (downtown) couldn't feel further apart. The former is the original stronghold from which the rest of the city expanded in the mid-13th century; the latter, to the north, is a wealthy district that flourished in the 18th century.

The cobbled, lantern-lit streets of Gamla Stan contained the administrative centre and much of the population until the 18th century. It is home to the Royal Palace and the Riksdagshuset, and visitors can enjoy leisurely ambles along fairytale alleyways lined with quaint bars, restaurants and shops. But it hasn't always been so picturesque: it was neglected in the 20th century and many of its houses fell into dilapidation, with some demolished for the expansion of the parliament building. Thankfully the need to preserve such heritage was recognised and the islet has been restored to its original splendour.

In Norrmalm, most residents were affluent merchants and the buildings closest to the waterfront – grand baroque and neoclassical structures – reflect this. In the 1930s the socialist government's regeneration project gave rise to the Konserthuset, Hötorgsskraporna and Kulturhuset. But besides the elegant architecture and cultural outlets you'll find the city's mercantile heart still thudding on in the form of great shops.

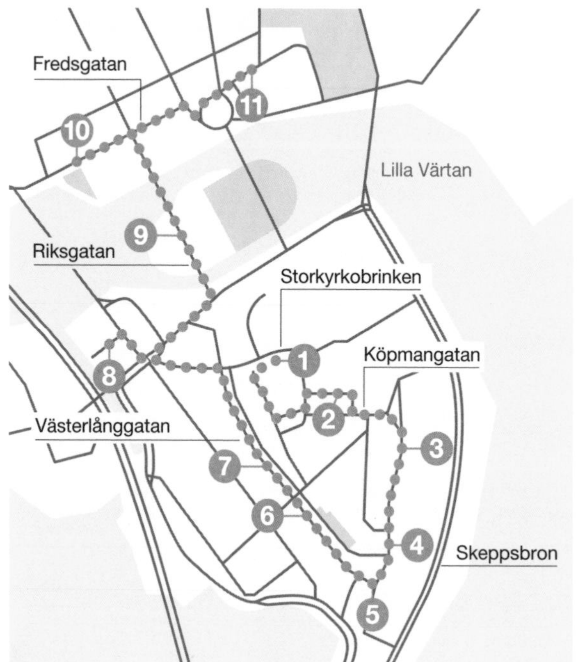

History, shops and culture
Gamla Stan and Norrmalm walk

Start at the mid-13th-century ① *Storkyrkan* cathedral, which was remodelled from 1736 to 1742 in the Italian baroque style. Inside you'll find the painting "Vädersolstavlan", the oldest known depiction of the city. The 1535 original is sadly lost but the canvas before you is a faithful copy from 1636. Exit onto Trångsund, head left and turn left again onto Stortorget, Gamla Stan's main square. Cross, take a

Getting there

Gamla Stan is easily reached by foot or metro (it's one stop from Central Station and another stop in the opposite direction from Slussen). Or hop onto one of the many buses stopping at Skeppsbron, the waterfront boulevard on the eastern side of the islet.

left onto Källagränd and then an immediate right. You'll come to eyewear brand 2 *Vasuma*, where friends Jan, Lars and Steffen make sleek specs for all occasions.

Exit right, take the first right again and then a left at Köpmangatan. When you reach a statue of Saint George and the Dragon head to your right down the sloping path onto the street below. Soon you'll hit 3 *Eye Shut Island*: a toy shop that's chock-full of prints and stationery (try the funky synthesisers from local firm Teenage Engineering).

Exit left and stretch your legs for a six-block stint before lunch at 4 *Den Gyldene Freden*. The 18th-century restaurant is one of the country's best known, famous as much for hosting the Nobel Academy's weekly dinners (every Thursday) as for its traditional dishes. Save room for dessert.

Exit left and take the second right onto Västerlånggatan, where you'll find 5 *Sundbergs Konditori*. It's believed to be the oldest café-bakery in Stockholm, dating back to 1785, and the fruit and custard tarts are the highlight. Next head to your right and 100 metres along, nip into 6 *Happy Socks*. Then continue to 7 *Designfirman Gamla Stan*, part of a series of design shops in the area that stock homeware, furniture and accessories by Scandi designers (the stoneware coffee-maker by Muuto is notable).

Exit left and proceed for some 150 metres before taking a left at Storkyrkobrinken. At the intersection, cross over to Riddarhusgränd and then turn left into the gardens of the 8 *Riddarhuset*. This 17th-century peach-hued palace was the political chamber of the Swedish nobles, equivalent to the UK's House of Lords (although the hereditary Swedish nobility play no official role in politics). Today it's the aristocracy's cultural and royal archive, and the seat of the Stockholm Philharmonic Orchestra.

Retrace your steps and take a left at the main road. Walk until the buildings clear and you can take the bridge over to Helgeandsholmen, the islet housing the 9 *Riksdagshuset*. The 1889 baroque-revival building once housed the Bank of Sweden, as well as parliament. Continue on and cross the bridge to Norrmalm, then take the second left. Near the steps to the Royal Academy of Fine Arts is 10 *Galleri Gunnar Olsson*, which has been showing abstract contemporary art for more than 40 years. Exit left and continue on, crossing the large square to reach Gustav Adolfs torg for a leisurely tipple at the reliably charming (and unambiguously named) 11 *Stockholm Wine Bar*.

Address book

01 Storkyrkan
1 Trångsund, 111 29
+46 (0)8 723 3000
stockholmsdomkyrkoforsamling.se

02 Vasuma
4 Trädgårdstvärgränd, 111 31
+46 (0)8 207 724
vasuma.com

03 Eye Shut Island
25 Österlånggatan, 111 31
+46 (0)7 0749 0128
eyeshutisland.com

04 Den Gyldene Freden
51 Österlånggatan, 111 31
+46 (0)8 249 760
gyldenefreden.se

05 Sundbergs Konditori
83 Järntorget, 111 29
+46 (0)8 106 735

06 Happy Socks
65 Västerlånggatan, 111 29
+46 (0)8 611 8702
happysocks.com

07 Designfirman Gamla Stan
40 Västerlånggatan, 111 29
+46 (0)7 0713 5573
designfirman.com

08 Riddarhuset
10 Riddarhustorget, 111 28
+46 (0)8 723 3990
riddarhuset.se

09 Riksdagshuset
1 Riksgatan, 100 12
+46 (0)8 786 4000
riksdagen.se

10 Galleri Gunnar Olsson
12 Fredsgatan, 111 52
+46 (0)8 210 777
olssongallery.com

11 Stockholm Wine Bar
16 Gustav Adolfs torg, 111 52
+46 (0)8 6841 8200
stockholmwinebar.se

NEIGHBOURHOOD 02

Vasastan

Artsy makeover

Vasastaden (simply Vasastan to those in the know) is named after Gustav Vasa, Sweden's first king. But despite its royal pedigree, it hasn't always been the well-to-do affair that it is today. During the 19th century, after the country saw a slump in fortune following its costly involvement in the Napoleonic wars (1803 to 1815), development of the quarter came to a halt. Fashionable couples in gilded carriages were replaced by down-and-outs, hovels and the occasional squabbling drunk.

By the 1880s a new plan was made to revive Vasastan: buildings went up, boulevards were widened, trees were planted and prosperity peaked as wealthy families started calling it home. The planners followed the classical 17th-century blueprints, resulting in a simple grid layout that still makes for easy navigation.

Today the neighbourhood is coveted by artsy middle-class Stockholmers thanks to its pleasant mix of lively restaurants, decent shops and cultural institutions (the area around Hudiksvallsgatan is the city's gallery district). It also offers some notable parks that are full of life from spring to autumn: Bellevueparken to the north, bordering Lake Brunnsviken, and Vasaparken, which lies a short walk from Gunnar Asplund's 1928 Stadsbibliotek.

Tranquil wandering

Vasastan walk

Start with a late-morning coffee and pastry at 1 *Nybergs Konditori*: the marzipan-and-vanilla princess cake is rightly raved about. Exit left onto Upplandsgatan and continue to the end of the block. On the right-hand corner is a curious old spot called 2 *Militär Ekiperings Aktiebolaget*, a court and military-dress tailor that has been kitting out guests for royal galas since 1883. Continue down the street and take

the third left onto Kammakargatan. Halfway up on your right is 3 *Lovalot*, which specialises in colourful clothing. A few steps further is 4 *Cask & Company*: the barware specialist stocks a range of weighty tumbler glasses, copper shakers and all the other trimmings for a shipshape home bar.

Exit to the left and continue past the baroque church on your right, until you reach a square crowned by the red-green 5 *Sankt Johannes Kyrka*. Construction plans for the church started in the late 18th century but the works never began, as the then king was dissatisfied with the blueprints. It would be another century before architect Carl Möller completed the gothic-revival structure.

Leave the square through the eastern side, along the street that passes by the Stockholm International School. Head down the stairs and turn right at the end of the alleyway onto Regeringsgatan: a smart central boulevard lined with ritzy restaurants with red ropes and a few high-end shops. Heading

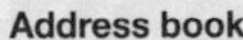

south, take the first left and you'll find 6 *Snickarbacken 7*. At this café, gallery and concept shop you can grab homeware, stationery and jewellery, before refuelling with an Asian salmon-and-quinoa salad (for something heartier, try the steak on rye).

Exit and retrace your steps, turning right at Regeringsgatan. Head up the street for a few blocks, continuing when the road merges with Birger Jarlsgatan, until you reach the brutalist Immanuelskyrkan (an angular concrete church). Turn left onto Kungstensgatan, then right onto Tulegatan. One block up (through the archway at number 19) is 7 *Elastic Gallery*, where curator Ola Gustafsson exhibits works by a roster of young Nordic artists. Always colourful and always free.

Exit left and you'll soon come to an enormous late-19th-century red-brick building. What looks like a royal palace is 8 *Norra Real*, the oldest secondary school in Stockholm and a far cry from the drab structures that most pupils are used to. Continue

along the street and turn right on intersecting Odengatan, crossing to the far side. Take the next left onto Roslagsgatan. On the second block along is Scandi-Japanese homeware shop 9 *Betonggruvan*, where designer and owner Josefine Halfwordson stocks porcelain bowls, colourful kitchen knives and her own furniture.

Continue and take the third left up the stairs into 10 *Vanadislunden*. Climb to the centre of the park for a splendid view of Stockholm to the south and the sprawling Lake Brunnsviken. The fortress-like structure behind you is not a high-security prison but a water-storage facility. Head for the southern exit that leads onto Döbelnsgatan, then take the next left.

Don't worry if you are thirsty: relief is close by. At the upcoming corner of Surbrunnsgatan and Tulegatan is 11 *Svartengrens*, a no-nonsense bar and restaurant serving an ever-changing menu of cocktails. Carnivores rejoice: generous cuts of steak are the house speciality.

Getting there

Odenplan is the nearest metro station to where the walk begins in Vasastan. Alternatively, take bus 61 to Dalagatan, which lies two blocks west of Nybergs Konditori.

Address book

01 **Nybergs Konditori**
26 Upplandsgatan, 113 60
+46 (0)8 321 195
nybergshembageri.se

02 **Militär Ekiperings Aktiebolaget**
23 Upplandsgatan, 113 60
+46 (0)8 348 501
nyamea.com

03 **Lovalot**
27 Kammakargatan, 111 60
lovalot.se

04 **Cask & Company**
42 Kammakargatan, 111 60
+46 (0)8 256 649
caskcompany.com

05 **Sankt Johannes Kyrka**
21 Johannesgatan, 111 38
+46 (0)8 5088 8650
svenskakyrkan.se

06 **Snickarbacken 7**
7 Snickarbacken, 111 39
+46 (0)8 6842 9009
snickarbacken7.se

07 **Elastic Gallery**
19 Tulegatan, 113 53
+46 (0)70 656 4319
elasticgallery.com

08 **Norra Real**
1 Roslagsgatan, 113 55
+46 (0)8 5083 2300
norrareal.stockholm.se

09 **Betonggruvan**
25 Roslagsgatan, 113 55
+46 (0)8 396 510
betonggruvan.se

10 **Vanadislunden**
Roslagsgatan, 113 54

11 **Svartengrens**
24 Tulegatan, 113 53
+46 (0)8 612 6550
svartengrens.se

NEIGHBOURHOOD 03

Södermalm
Southern belle

Södermalm – Söder for short – lies just south of Gamla Stan. You reach the island via Slussen, the watergate that separates Lake Mälaren to the west of the island from the Baltic Sea on the east. The island-borough fell under Stockholm's rule in 1436 in response to the city's sudden growth and until the 19th century it was primarily used as farmland. That changed once a railway was introduced in 1860. From that year forward, Söder became Stockholm's working-class neighbourhood and today it remains one of the last places in the capital where 18th-century wooden houses and industrial architecture can be found.

Gentrification hit by the late 20th century and turned what was once a shabby district into one of the city's most dynamic areas. Its transformation was helped by pop-culture references, such as the late Swedish author Stieg Larsson's Millennium trilogy, which is set here. Over the years the district – which is the birthplace of Hollywood actress Greta Garbo – has become known as the Soho of Stockholm, so much so that the area south of Folkungagatan has been nicknamed Sofo.

To the west of Sofo is Götgatan, one of Söder's main arteries, and along here is Medborgarplatsen, the popular meeting place where this walk will begin.

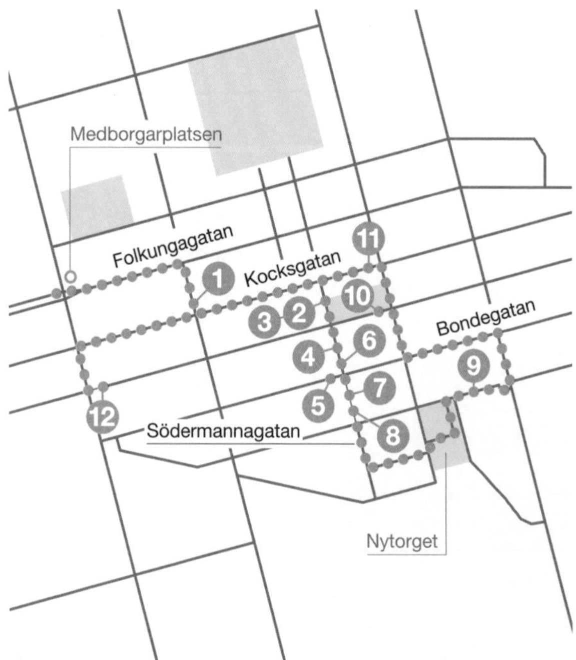

Music, meatballs and more
Södermalm walk

Begin this walk at city square Medborgarplatsen and wander east along Folkungagatan. Hang a right at Östgötagatan and make your way to ❶ *K17*, a menswear shop that stocks brands such as Hansen and Andersen-Andersen, and hosts live music performances on the last Thursday of every month.

Grab a pair of comfortable trainers at ❷ *Gram Shoes*. You will get there by turning left

onto Kocksgatan and right onto Södermannagatan, opposite leafy Axel Landquists Park. Next door to the shoe shop is ❸ *Galleri Axel*, a contemporary photo gallery run by photographer Bea Tigerhielm.

Head down Södermannagatan until you reach ❹ *The English Bookshop*, which imports English-language publications from the UK and US every week and has many cosy corners in which to curl up with a book. Once back outside keep following the road until you hit a traditional Falu-red house. Inside the wooden hut you'll find an old-school pottery workshop known as ❺ *Krukmakeriet*, where Anne Junsjö fashions one-of-a-kind ceramics and homeware. The building diagonally across the road offers quite a contrast: a stately house that dates from 1889. Above its arched entrance you'll find the letters J-U-L-I-U-S, spelling the name of Julius Westerdahl, the man who opened Öhmans bakery here in the 19th century. Some say he invented the Scandinavian-style crisp bread, known in Sweden as *knäckebröd*. Curious? Pass through

the gates and explore the old bakery, which has since been sold to Wasabröd and is now home to various studios, including a 6 *Vitra Showroom* that displays design classics by the likes of Charles and Ray Eames, Jasper Morrison and Alvar Aalto.

Once you've seen it all, return to Södermannagatan and drop into 7 *LA Bruket*, a skincare brand co-founded by ceramicist Monica Kylén. Further down the street on the corner of Södermannagatan and Skånegatan is 8 *Il Caffè*, which serves great coffee and delicious cinnamon buns – and the smell of fresh flowers from the attached florist is divine. Once the caffeine has kicked in, stroll through the small Nytorget Park and marvel at the colourful wooden cottages then continue on Skånegatan until you reach 9 *Kerber*, which sells timeless womenswear designed by Marielle Kerber (the brand's eye-catching identity was created by The Studio).

You can't visit Stockholm without stopping by 10 *Acne Studios*. The fashion house has a branch on Nytorgsgatan and the best way to get there is by turning left onto Renstiernas gata and left again on Bondegatan. Veer right at the next corner, walk 50 metres and voilà.

Take a well-deserved break at 11 *Meatballs for the People*, where Sweden's famous dish comes in a variety of guises, from moose to salmon, reindeer to rooster. Ingredients are sourced from regional farms and dishes are served with potato purée, lingonberries and gravy. Its slogan? "Two balls a day keeps the doctor away." Alternatively you may want to try Greasy Spoon (our top pick for brunch) two blocks up from here at Tjärhovsgatan 19.

Ready for dessert? Head over to 12 *Victoria Cinema* for popcorn and an arthouse film; its bright-red neon sign is hard to miss. The fastest way to get there is by walking down Kocksgatan in the direction of Medborgarplatsen. But instead of turning right on Götgatan, which would take you back to where you started, turn left and follow the bright lights.

Getting there

Hop on either the 17, 18 or 19 subway lines to Medborgarplatsen. Alternatively, hitch a ride on the 66, 193, 194, 195, 791 or 794 buses.

Address book

01 K17
17 Kocksgatan, 116 24
+46 (0)8 4205 7398
k17.se

02 Gram Shoes
16 Södermannagatan, 116 23
+46 (0)7 2013 6973
gramshoes.com

03 Galleri Axel
16 Södermannagatan, 116 23
+46 (0)7 3591 9136
galleriaxel.se

04 The English Bookshop
22 Södermannagatan, 116 23
+46 (0)8 790 5510
bookshop.se

05 Krukmakeriet
32 Bondegatan, 116 33
+46 (0)7 3980 0593
annejunsjo.se

06 Vitra Showroom
21 Bondegatan, 116 33
vitra.com

07 LA Bruket
19 Södermannagatan, 116 40
+46 (0)8 615 0011
labruket.se

08 Il Caffè
23 Södermannagatan, 116 40
+46 (0)8 462 9500
ilcaffe.se

09 Kerber
83 Skånegatan, 116 35
+46 (0)7 3045 7711
kerber.se

10 Acne Studios
36 Nytorgsgatan, 116 40
+46 (0)8 640 0470
acnestudios.com

11 Meatballs for the People
30 Nytorgsgatan, 116 40
+46 (0)8 466 6099
meatball.se

12 Victoria Cinema
67 Götgatan, 116 21
+46 (0)8 5626 0000
svenskabio.se

NEIGHBOURHOOD 04

Östermalm

Barn conversion

Östermalm may feel established but it's a relatively young part of the city. The district only dates back to the 19th century, when wide boulevards inspired by Haussmann's Paris were built across the boggy shores – the most prominent of which is Strandvägen, which stretches along the waterfront with views of Djurgården and Stockholm's museum island. At the boulevard's western end is the 19th-century Dramaten (Royal Dramatic Theatre) on Nybroplan, which is where Birger Jarlsgatan begins and European fashion houses such as Prada and Louis Vuitton vie for customers.

The street – which passes by Humlegården, a park that's home to the Kungliga biblioteket (Sweden's national library) – is one of the city's longest and divides the neighbourhood in two. Historically Östermalm was reserved for the king's cattle (and military) and was known as Ladugårdslandet (Barn Land). It wasn't until late in the 19th century that the bourgeoisie built mansions along the waterfront and renamed the area.

But it's not just the rich and the fashion-conscious who have made a home here. It's also the centre of Sweden's media industry: national public TV and radio broadcasters are found alongside some of the city's finest independent retailers.

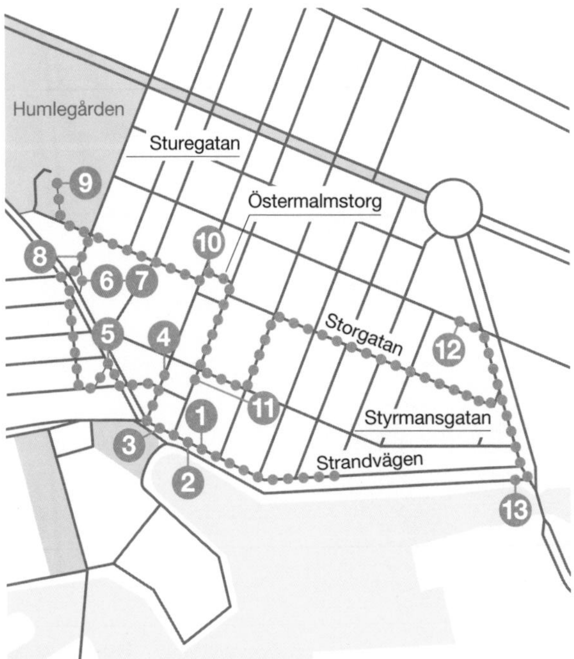

Lucky star
Östermalm walk

Begin your journey at the corner of Strandvägen and Styrmansgatan, walking west along the tree-lined boulevard, ringed by grand façades on one side and boats on the other, until you reach 1 *Malmstenbutiken*. Opened by Swedish designer Carl Malmsten in 1940, the shop showcases his collection of mid-century Nordic furniture, which includes the Lilla Åland chair and Visingsö bench.

Next door is 2 *Svenskt Tenn*, which has been displaying pieces by one of the fathers of Swedish modernism, Josef Frank (*see page 91*), among others since 1924.

Where Strandvägen ends and Nybroplan begins you'll find the 3 *Dramaten*, an art nouveau landmark and Sweden's national theatre. As you walk up Nybrogatan don't forget to rub the belly of the bronze sculpture of late actress Margaret Krook: it's good luck, we're told. Further up the road at number six, the smell of fresh bread will likely entice you into 4 *Fabrique*, a bakery that serves some of the best cinnamon buns in the city. Once out on the street again, turn back and make a right onto Ingmar Bergmans gata. When you reach the stately Birger Jarlsgatan, make your way towards Prada – not for their bags but because next door you'll find the beautiful 5 *Birger Jarlspassagen*, a shopping arcade designed by Ludvig Peterson, which opened in 1897.

Walk to the end of the black-and-white-tiled mall until you reach Deli & Wine by Carotte, a prime

spot at which to stop for a glass of wine. Once refreshed, step out onto Smålandsgatan and turn right, then right again. Follow the road until you reach Stureplan Square. Before entering the Sturegallerian, poke your head into 6 *Hedengrens* and lose yourself in its bewildering two-floor selection of books. Inside 7 *Sturegallerian* you'll find all kinds of shops but, as food is the best way to get to know a country, we recommend visiting the brasserie Sturehof, originally modelled on a German beer hall. Exit where you entered and turn right onto Sturegatan where you'll find 8 *Taverna Brillo*, another super choice for business lunches and dinners with friends and family. Further down the road you'll see Humlegården, an oasis that's home to the 9 *Kungliga biblioteket* as well as a statue of Swedish naturalist Carl Linnaeus (he brought us the binomial system that organises plants and species by name; without him we wouldn't be called Homo sapiens).

Head back to the road and, once on Humlegårdsgatan, turn left and continue until you reach the 10 *Östermalms Saluhall* (the original market hall dating from 1888 will reopen in 2018 but the temporary venue offers plentiful plates). Head towards the 18th-century Hedvig Eleonora Kyrka and turn right onto Sibyllegatan, past the Armémuseum and straight towards the Kronobageriet, the former home of the Crown Bakery and now site of the 11 *Swedish Museum of Performing Arts*.

Exit right and turn right again onto Riddargatan before turning left at Artillerigatan and right at Storgatan. Head straight until you reach Narvavägen, where you'll spot the large yellow-hued 12 *Historiska Museet* further north. Brush up on your history and return to Narvavägen and head downhill towards the water. If it's a sunny day, soak up the rays from the terrace of 13 *Strandbryggan* café or continue your journey onto museum island (Djurgården), where you'll find Skansen, the world's first open-air museum.

Getting there

The walk begins at Styrmansgatan and the fastest way to get there via public transport is by taking the bus (67, 69, 76) or tram (line 7). Or if the sun's out, why not walk or bike along the waterfront until you reach the starting point?

Address book

01 Malmstenbutiken
5B Strandvägen, 114 51
+46 (0)8 233 380
malmsten.se

02 Svenskt Tenn
5 Strandvägen, 114 51
+46 (0)8 670 1600
svenskttenn.se

03 Dramaten
Nybroplan, 111 47
+46 (0)8 667 0680
dramaten.se

04 Fabrique
6 Nybrogatan, 114 34
+46 (0)8 661 8300
fabrique.se

05 Birger Jarlspassagen
7-9 Birger Jarlsgatan, 111 46

06 Hedengrens
4 Stureplan, 114 85
+46 (0)8 611 5128
hedengrens.se

07 Sturegallerian
4 Stureplan, 114 35

08 Taverna Brillo
6 Sturegatan, 114 35
+46 (0)8 5197 7800
tavernabrillo.se

09 Kungliga biblioteket
26 Humlegårdsgatan, 102 41
+46 (0)1 0709 3000
kb.se

10 Östermalms Saluhall
Östermalmstorg, 114 39
ostermalmshallen.se

11 Swedish Museum of Performing Arts
2 Sibyllegatan, 114 51
+46 (0)8 5195 6700
scenkonstmuseet.se

12 Historiska Museet
13-17 Narvavägen, 114 84
+46 (0)8 5195 5600
historiska.se

13 Strandbryggan
27 Strandvägskajen, 114 56
strandbryggan.se

NEIGHBOURHOOD 05

Kungsholmen

Industrious island

Kungsholmen (King's Island) is the most residential and sleepy of Stockholm's central areas. On warm weekends, residents meander along the waterfront promenade, which affords stunning views of Södermalm and Lake Mälaren. Pair this with up-and-coming restaurants and some decent cafés in which to linger and you'll soon see why so many Swedes have moved here.

The current residents are just the latest wave. The first were Franciscan monks in the 15th century, although they were turfed out 100 years or so later and had their land confiscated. Next to move in were high-ranking officers in the 1600s, returning from the Thirty Years' War. The ex-soldiers built opulent estates on the west of the island, while vast swathes of land were put to use thanks to subsidies for artisans and manufacturers. In the 18th century, shortly after the collapse of the Swedish empire, the crown again showered Kungsholmen with economic incentives to increase its industrial clout, giving rise to cotton and porcelain factories. Prosperity led to a population boom and the number of residents increased almost sevenfold from 1860 to 1890.

Look beyond the Stadshuset on the island's eastern tip. From open-air film screenings in Rålambshovsparken to gems of functionalist architecture along Norr Mälarstrand, quiet but stately Kungsholmen is fast regaining its crown.

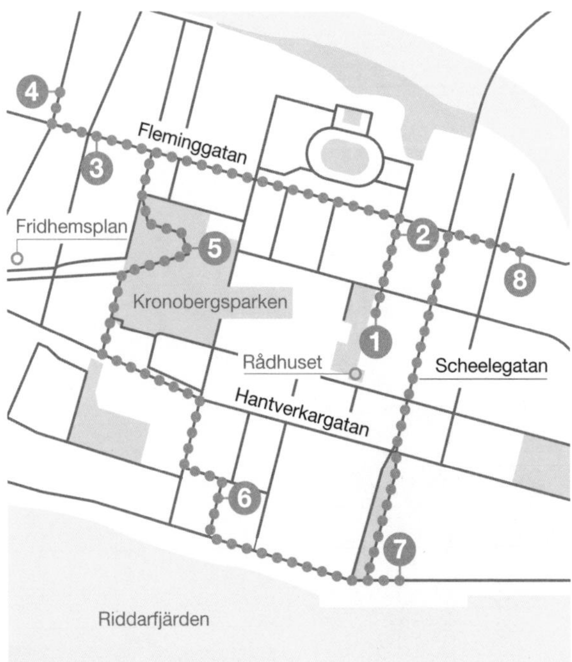

Parks and baked treats
Kungsholmen walk

Start outside the 1 *Stockholm Polishuset*, a palatial pale-yellow structure that was built in 1911 and criticised for its straight lines and austere look: the design broke with the swirly national romantic style popular during the era. Head north on the little footpath to Kungsholmsgatan; cross it and walk up Norra Agnegatan. At the end of the block you'll reach 2 *Lod*, where a band of Swedish

metal-workers have been fashioning all manner of jewellery and tasteful homeware since 1999.

Continue north on Norra Agnegatan and take the first left onto Fleminggatan. Continue up this main boulevard for six blocks. If you're in need of a pick-me-up stop at 3 *Fabrique* bakery on the corner of Fleminggatan and Sankt Eriksgatan for a coffee and a walnut bun. Then continue on for another block and turn right on Fridhemsgatan. On the left you'll come across the second site of men's and womenswear shop 4 *Grandpa* (the original is in Söder). The choice is extensive, from Velour by Nostalgi shirts to dresses by Stockholm-based Rodebjer, mingled with thick blankets from Low Key, plus prints and tableware.

Retrace your steps, returning to Fleminggatan, and turn left. Take the second right heading towards 5 *Kronobergsparken*. On the northern slope of the central hillock a steel statue, "A Modern Icarus" by Barbro Liljander, depicts a man about to take flight

on a glider. Climb to the top of the hill for views of Kungsholmen and the city.

Exit along the western side of the park and proceed left down Kronobergsgatan. Take the second left and look east down the street for a fine vista of the Stadshuset tower in the far distance, topped by a golden spire depicting the triple crown of the historic Kalmar Union (which united Sweden, Denmark and Norway).

Continue down the street in the direction of the tower and after one block whip right onto Polhemsgatan. Take the first left and then the first right to come to bakery 6 *Petite France*. The custard canelé is a delight but the chocolate-and-hazelnut pastry is even better. Grab it to go: there's plenty more to see.

Turn left out of the bakery and then take another left down Norr Mälarstrand. A few blocks down, after you've passed the tree-lined Kungsholmstorg Park, you'll find 7 *Folk & Friends*: a bar where you can sample some restorative draughts of beer and get a taste of the bubbling brewery scene. We recommend the Table Saison by the Stockholm Brewing Co, which is based in Södermalm.

After a few sips (or bottles, we're not judging) exit right and turn right again up Kungsholmstorg. As the two sides of the boulevard merge into Scheelegatan, keep heading straight. After a further five blocks, turn right onto Fleminggatan. Up ahead is restaurant 8 *Usine Ile Roi*, an offshoot of popular Södermalm bistro Usine (both serve European favourites). If you drop in at lunch, opt for the reasonably priced and constantly changing menu of specials: they're unerringly good.

Getting there

Kungsholmen is less than 30 minutes' walk from Gamla Stan, Norrmalm and Vasastan; the strikingly arched Västerbron connects the island to Södermalm. The closest metro stations to the starting point of the walk are Rådhuset and Fridhemsplan.

Address book

01 Stockholm Polishuset
48 Bergsgata, 112 31
+46 (0)7 7114 1400
polisen.se

02 Lod
40 Norra Agnegatan, 112 29
+46 (0)8 652 2228
lod.nu

03 Fabrique
83 Fleminggatan, 112 33
+46 (0)8 650 0044
fabrique.se

04 Grandpa
43 Fridhemsgatan, 112 46
+46 (0)8 643 6081
grandpa.se

05 Kronobergsparken
Kungsholmen, 112 38

06 Petite France
6 John Ericssonsgatan, 112 22
petitefrance.se
+46 (0)8 618 2800

07 Folk & Friends
32 Norr Mälarstrand, 112 20
+46 (0)7 6321 7442
folk.beer

08 Usine Ile Roi
7 Fleminggatan, 112 26
+46 (0)8 1205 1336
usine.se

Resources
—— Inside knowledge

We've told you the best places to eat and drink, what cultural sights to see and which museums to mooch around. We've also shared our favourite neighbourhoods to stroll through, the top shopping spots and even where to get your fitness hit.

Now all you need is that special something to make Stockholm truly accessible: local knowledge. Whether you want to ask someone out for a coffee, need to buy a bus ticket or are stuck for something to do when it rains, it's all here. Check out our insider tips on getting around, dance through the streets to our top-five tunes and take advantage of the best events taking place in this eclectic city.

Transport
Get around town

01 **Walk:** Stockholm is smaller than it appears; it only takes an hour to get from north to south. Just check the bridges you intend to cross and watch out for the uneven cobblestones in Gamla Stan.

02 **Metro:** Stockholm's three lines cover seven routes and 100 stations. It works well but prices are steep: a one-way ticket is SEK43 so get a three or seven-day pass if you're around for longer, costing SEK240 and SEK315 respectively. Buy tickets at metro stations, Pressbyrån or 7-11 shops.
sl.se

03 **Boats:** It's not called "The Venice of the North" for nothing. Most ferries run between Slussen in Gamla Stan and Nybroplan in Norrmalm to the archipelago but there are some internal routes, such as the boat to Djurgården. One-way tickets start at SEK79.
waxholmsbolaget.se

04 **Buses:** Buses are speedy, clean, rarely packed and stop at well-thought-out intervals. You can buy tickets, which again are expensive at SEK43 for a one-way journey, from metro stops and convenience stores.
sl.se

05 **Trams:** Route S7, the one and only, runs from Central Station through to Djurgården. It shortens travel time for those heading to the eastern island.
djurgardslinjen.se

06 **Flights:** Arlanda is the main airport for international flights and is easy to get to using the Arlanda Express (there's also Bromma for domestic flights). Tickets can be bought online or at machines near the platform. Take care not to use a standard ticket dispenser elsewhere in town: this is for the slow train.
swedavia.com

Vocabulary
Local lingo

Most Swedes speak English (demurely but faultlessly) but they'll be impressed (or at worst amused) if you throw in a few local phrases.

01 **Förlåt:** Sorry
02 **Härligt:** Wonderful
03 **Hej:** Hello
04 **Hejdå:** Goodbye
05 **Lagom:** Not too little, not too much
06 **Precis:** Exactly
07 **Ska vi fika:** Shall we have a coffee?
08 **Skål:** Cheers
09 **Ta det lugnt:** Take it easy
10 **Tack:** Thank you

Soundtrack to the city
Five top tunes

01 **Franz Berwald, 'Sinfonie Sérieuse':** The Stockholm-born composer practised as a surgeon and worked in a factory before releasing this heartfelt paean to the Swedish landscape in 1842.

02 **Abba, 'Dancing Queen':** Yes it's silly but what's a round-up of Stockholm's music without Abba? You'll change your tune at 03.00 in Bar Riche.

03 **Monica Zetterlund, 'Sakta Vi Gå Genom Stan':** Jazz star Zetterlund's 1962 adaption of "Walking My Baby Home" is an old favourite.

04 **Eagle-Eye Cherry, 'Save Tonight':** Feel-good rock about the daily happenings in 1990s Södermalm: a butcher gets robbed, an eager suitor prepares for a date and life goes on.

05 **Emilia de Poret, 'Mistreat me (You'll Be Sorry)':** The Swedish pop sensation's debut single, released under the name Lia Andreen, hit CD players in 2001 and earned her the unofficial moniker of Sweden's Britney Spears, not least for the feisty lyrics.

Best events
What to see

01 **Stockholm Fashion Week, citywide:** It may be an invite-only affair but just grab a window seat at a café and watch the streets turn into one long catwalk.
January, fashionweek.se

02 **Stockholm Design Week, citywide:** The biggest design fair in Scandinavia. The industry's cognoscenti – plus its share of dilettantes – descend on the city for a good time and, while the fair itself takes place outside Stockholm, there are many public exhibitions and events to be enjoyed (as well as parties to crash).
February, stockholmdesignweek.com

03 **Walpurgis Night, Djurgården:** A nationwide night of bonfires, drinking and singing to welcome spring (and ward off evil spirits, of course). May Day, the day after, sees parades around town as King Carl XVI Gustaf celebrates his birthday (which, confusingly, is on 30 April).
30 April to 1 May

04 **Midsummer, citywide:** Many don traditional outfits and florid wreaths, sing folk songs and drink schnapps to celebrate the longest day of the year. Some families will head out into the countryside but the celebrations in town, especially on rooftop terraces such as Mosebacke, are equally heartfelt.
June

05 **National Day, Skansen and Skeppsbron:** Skansen, a zoo and open-air museum of Swedish heritage, welcomes the royal family for a day of pageantry to celebrate the election of Sweden's first king, Gustav Vasa. Everyone then heads over to Skeppsbron outside the royal palace for the release of 50,000 blue and yellow balloons (the colours of the Swedish flag, as you won't have failed to notice).
6 June, sweden.se

06 **Pride Week, Södermalm:** The city's trendy southern island hosts a week-long celebration of LGBT culture, the biggest such event in Scandinavia. There are events around town but most of the festivities take place in Pride Park in Södermalm, which hosts everything from live music and debates to film screenings and food markets.
July to August, stockholmpride.org

07 **Midnattsloppet, Södermalm:** Participants (16,000) and revellers (200,000) descend on Södermalm for an evening 10km run followed by live music and parties. There is also a 2km course for the youngsters.
August, midnattsloppet.com

08 **Summer Cinema, Rålambshovsparken:** A free five-day outdoor cinema event. Films tend to be the top picks from the most recent Stockholm Film Festival and always in the original language. Be sure to bring blankets and a bottle of something warming.
August, stockholmfilmfestival.se

09 **Stockholm Beer & Whiskey Festival, Nacka Strand:** This celebration spans two weekends and takes place at the Nacka Strandmässan Factory just outside central Stockholm. On offer are some 500 beers, ciders and whiskies from Stockholm, Sweden and beyond.
September to October, stockholmbeer.se

10 **Stockholm International Film Festival, citywide:** From big premieres to small indie affairs, screenings take place in cinemas throughout town. The events are open to all. Tickets start at SEK170 and can be purchased at the Kulturhuset.
November to December, stockholmfilmfestival.se

Sunny days
The great outdoors

01 **Hagaparken:** A great sprawling space by Lake Brunnsviken that's large enough to throw a frisbee around without upsetting people. Rent a rowing boat or simply sunbathe.

02 **Walk around Kungsholmen waterfront:** A typical pastime among Kungsholmen's residents (younger families and a more understated set than those on the south island). The southern waterfront (Norr Mälarstrand) offers a great vista of Södermalm. We even spotted a few dapper souls dressed up to the nines in their Sunday best for the stroll.

03 **Rooftop terraces:** Forget *fika* (for a minute), this is arguably the capital's pastime of choice. Usually accompanied by good live music and close friends.

Rainy days
Weather-proof activities

01 **Cafés:** In Sweden, cafés are more than coffee stops: they're a place of respite and socialising. So don't just gobble that bun and run off. Cosy up on the sofa with a pal – or work up the courage to talk to someone who you've got your eye on.

02 **Baking:** Instead of just scoffing the cinnamon buns, why not take home the know-how needed to make them? Dodge the puddles and head for Norrmalm, where The Pastry Studio will teach you how to bake traditional pastries.
thepastrystudio.se

03 **Churches:** Yes, they lack the regalia and artwork of Italy (you're a spoiled lot) but the charm lies in their austerity and varied styles, from rococo to boxy national romanticism.

About Monocle
Step inside

In 2007, Monocle was launched as a monthly magazine briefing on global affairs, business, culture, design and much more. We believed there was a globally minded audience of readers who were hungry for opportunities and experiences beyond their national borders.

Today Monocle is a complete media brand with print, audio and online elements – not to mention our expanding network of shops and cafés. Besides our London HQ we have seven international bureaux in New York, Toronto, Istanbul, Singapore, Tokyo, Zürich and Hong Kong. We continue to grow and flourish and at our core is the simple belief that there will always be a place for a print brand that is committed to telling fresh stories and sending photographers on assignments. It's also a case of knowing that our success is all down to the readers, advertisers and collaborators who have supported us along the way.

London HQ
Our editorial office is in Marylebone

1
International bureaux
Boots on the ground

We have an HQ in London and call upon firsthand reports from our contributors in more than 35 cities around the world. We also have seven international bureaux. For this travel guide, MONOCLE reporters Josh Fehnert, Melkon Charchoglyan, Marie-Sophie Schwarzer and Jamie Waters decamped to Stockholm to explore all that it has to offer. They also called on the assistance of writers in the city, as well as our correspondent Elna Nykänen-Andersson, to ensure that we have covered the best in retail, food, hospitality and entertainment. The aim is to make you feel like a local in the Swedish capital.

Online
Digital delivery

We have a dynamic website: *monocle.com*. As well as being the place to hear our radio station, Monocle 24, the site presents our films, which are beautifully shot and edited by our in-house team and provide a fresh perspective on our stories. Check out the films celebrating the cities that make up our Travel Guide Series before you explore the rest of the site.

Retail and cafés
Food for thought

Via our shops in Hong Kong, Toronto, New York, Tokyo, London and Singapore we sell products that cater to our readers' tastes and are produced in collaboration with brands we believe in. We also have cafés in Tokyo and London. And if you are in the UK capital visit the Kioskafé in Paddington, which combines good coffee and great reads.

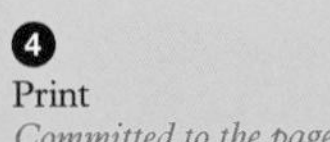

Print

Committed to the page

MONOCLE is published 10 times a year. We have stayed loyal to our belief in quality print with two extra seasonal publications: THE FORECAST, packed with key insights into the year ahead, and THE ESCAPIST, our summer travel-minded magazine. To sign up visit *monocle.com/subscribe*. Since 2013 we have also been publishing books, like this one, in partnership with Gestalten.

5

Radio

Sound approach

Monocle 24 is our round-the-clock radio station that was launched in 2011. It delivers global news and shows covering foreign affairs, urbanism, business, culture, food and drink, design and print media. When you find yourself in Stockholm tune into *The Globalist*, our morning news programme that is the perfect way to start the day in Europe. We also have a playlist to accompany you day and night, regularly assisted by live band sessions that are hosted at our Midori House headquarters in London. You can listen live or download any of our shows from *monocle.com*, iTunes or SoundCloud.

Priority service

Subscribers save 10 per cent in our online shop

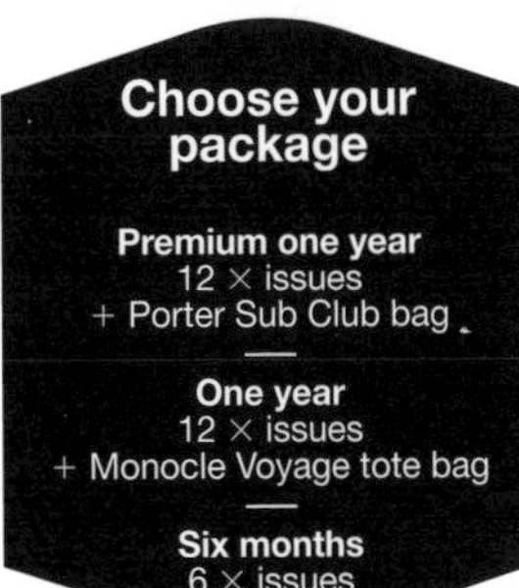

Choose your package

Premium one year
12 × issues
+ Porter Sub Club bag

One year
12 × issues
+ Monocle Voyage tote bag

Six months
6 × issues

Join the club

01
Subscribe to Monocle
A subscription is a simple way to make sure that you never miss an issue – and you'll enjoy many additional benefits.

02
Be in the know
Our subscribers have exclusive access to the entire Monocle archive and priority access to selected product collaborations at *monocle.com*.

03
Stay in the loop
Subscription copies are delivered to your door at no extra cost no matter where you are in the world. We also offer an auto-renewal service to ensure that you never miss an issue.

04
And there's more...
Subscribers benefit from a 10 per cent discount at all Monocle shops, including online, and receive exclusive offers and invitations to events around the world.

Writers
Jan Arnald
Fernando Augusto Pacheco
Anna Brones
Beatrice Carmi
Melkon Charchoglyan
Josh Fehnert
Stella Friberg
Tom Furse
Naomi Jones
Daphne Karnezis
Andreas Martin-Löf
Saskia Neumann
Elna Nykänen Andersson
Marie-Sophie Schwarzer
Jamie Waters
Stephen Whitlock

Chief photographer
Simon Bajada

Still life
David Sykes

Images
Felix Odell
Peter Berg
Olle Broksten
Åke E:son Lindman
Dag Granath
Martin Isaksson
Johan Lygrell
Jonatan Låstbom
Per Levander
Adam Lewenhaupt
Idha Lindhag
Sarah Lönn
Magnus Skoglöf
Johan Wennerström

Illustrators
Satoshi Hashimoto
Ceylan Sahin Eker
Tokuma

Monocle
EDITOR IN CHIEF AND CHAIRMAN
Tyler Brûlé
EDITOR
Andrew Tuck
CREATIVE DIRECTOR
Richard Spencer Powell

The Monocle Travel Guide Series: Stockholm

GUIDE EDITOR
Josh Fehnert
ASSOCIATE GUIDE EDITORS
Melkon Charchoglyan
Marie-Sophie Schwarzer
Jamie Waters
PHOTO EDITOR
Victoria Cagol

The Monocle Travel Guide Series

SERIES EDITOR
Joe Pickard
ASSOCIATE EDITOR
Chloë Ashby
ASSISTANT EDITOR
Mikaela Aitken
RESEARCHER
Melkon Charchoglyan
DESIGNERS
Maria Hamer
Loi Xuan Ly
Jay Yeo
PHOTO EDITORS
Matthew Beaman
Victoria Cagol
Shin Miura

PRODUCTION
Jacqueline Deacon
Dan Poole
Rachel Kurzfield
Sean McGeady
Sonia Zhuravlyova

CHAPTER EDITING

Need to know
Josh Fehnert

Hotels
Josh Fehnert

Food and drink
Josh Fehnert
Melkon Charchoglyan

Retail
Jamie Waters

Things we'd buy
Josh Fehnert
Melkon Charchoglyan

Essays
Joe Pickard
Melkon Charchoglyan

Culture
Melkon Charchoglyan

Design and architecture
Marie-Sophie Schwarzer

Sport and fitness
Jamie Waters

Walks
Melkon Charchoglyan

Resources
Melkon Charchoglyan

Research
Beatrice Carmi
Melkon Charchoglyan
Tom Furse
Naomi Jones
Daphne Karnezis
Ian Keddie
Maria Kitano
Charles MacFarlane
Fabian Mayer
Ceinwen Thomas
Steven Whitlock
Zayana Zulkiflee

Special thanks
Helene Boström
Ebba Bozorgnia
Frederik Carlström
Emilia de Poret
Richard Feigin
Stella Friberg
Andrea Ingvar
Pete Kempshall
Jesper King
Mats Klingberg
Andreas Martin-Löf
PG Nilsson
Elna Nykänen Andersson
Emma Ohlson
Alex Olsson
Ulrika Pilo
Sabina von Greyerz
Erica Wigge

New

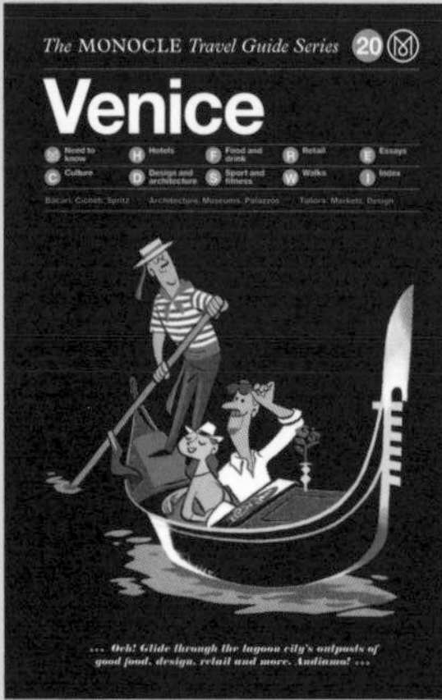

The collection

We hope you have found the Monocle Travel Guide to Stockholm useful, inspiring and entertaining. There's plenty more to get your teeth into: we have a global suite of guides, with many more set to be released in the coming months. Cities are fun. Let's explore.

1 London
The sights, sounds and style

2 New York
Get a taste of the Big Apple's best

3 Tokyo
The enigmatic glory of Japan's capital

4 Hong Kong
Down to business in this vibrant city

5 Madrid
Captivating capital abuzz with spirit

6 Bangkok
Stimulate your senses with the exotic

7 Istanbul
Thrilling fusion of Asia and Europe

8 Miami
Unpack the Magic City's box of tricks

9 Rio de Janeiro
Beaches, bars and bossa nova

10 Paris
Be romanced by the City of Light

11 Singapore
Where modernity meets tradition

12 Vienna
Waltz through the Austrian capital

13 Sydney
Sun, surf and urban delights

14 Honolulu
Embrace Hawaii's aloha spirit

15 Copenhagen
Cycle through the Danish capital

16 Los Angeles
Fly high in the City of Angels

17 Toronto
Delve into this diverse Canadian city

18 Berlin
Discover the city of two halves

19 Rome
Scoot through the Eternal City

20 Venice
Wonder at the waterways

21 Amsterdam
Canals, bicycles and liberalism

22 Stockholm
Sweden's suave, charming capital